MW01054342

Building Modern Serverless Web APIs

Develop Microservices and Implement Serverless Applications with .NET Core 3.1 and AWS Lambda

Tanmoy Sarkar

www.bpbonline.com

Distributors:

BPB PUBLICATIONS
20, Ansari Road, Darya Ganj
New Delhi-110002
Ph: 23254990/23254991

DECCAN AGENCIES
4-3-329, Bank Street,
Hyderabad-500195
Ph: 24756967/24756400

MICRO MEDIA
Shop No. 5, Mahendra Chambers,
150 DN Rd. Next to Capital Cinema,
V.T. (C.S.T.) Station, MUMBAI-400 001
Ph: 22078296/22078297

BPB BOOK CENTRE
376 Old Lajpat Rai Market,
Delhi-110006
Ph: 23861747

To View Complete
BPB Publications Catalogue
Scan the QR Code:

Published by Manish Jain for BPB Publications, 20 Ansari Road, Darya Ganj, New Delhi-110002 and Printed by him at Repro India Ltd, Mumbai

Dedicated to

My respected elders,
My wife Niva,
and
Tanistha Sarkar
My daughter, who has been an angel in my life.

About the Author

Tanmoy Sarkar is an AWS Solutions Architect - Associate certified professional offering experience of more than 11 years in the IT industry. He has handled responsibilities as a Lead in application design, development, and support on enterprise application integration and Microsoft technologies. He is currently working as a Senior Consultant in Neudesic LLC, Hyderabad, India.

Tanmoy Sakar holds a Master's degree in Distributed and Mobile Computing (Gold Medalist) from Jadavpur University, Kolkata and has published papers in national and international conferences

About the Reviewer

Rishabh Verma is a Microsoft-certified professional and works at Microsoft as a Senior Development Consultant, helping the customers to design, develop, and deploy enterprise-level applications. An Electronic Engineer by education, he has 13+ years of hardcore development experience on the .NET technology stack. He has authored books on .NET Core 2.0, .NET Core 3.1, parallel programming and Visual Studio Extensibility Development. He is passionate about creating tools, Visual Studio extensions, and utilities to increase developer productivity. His interests are .NET Compiler Platform (Roslyn), Visual Studio extensibility, code generation and .NET Core. In his leisure time, he writes technical articles, tools and utilities, reviews codes, and conducts talks in technical communities. He has conducted talks, sessions, and workshops both inside as well as outside Microsoft and has been a speaker in prestigious global conferences. He is a member of .NET foundation (**https://dotnetfoundation.org/community/speakers/ rishabh-verma**). He occasionally blogs at **https://rishabhverma.net/**. His twitter id is @VermaRishabh and his LinkedIn page is **https://www.linkedin.com/in/ rishabhverma/**

Acknowledgement

There are a few people I want to thank for the continued and ongoing support they gave me while writing this book. First and foremost, I would like to thank my wife, Niva Das, and my little daughter, Tanistha for putting up with me while I spent many weekends and evenings on writing. —I could have never completed this book without their support.

Finally, I would like to thank BPB Publications for their constant support and for helping me to write my first book.

Preface

Nowadays, microservices are the new standards to host backend applications because of their language-agnostic, resiliency, and loosely coupled nature. It can be developed independently by different teams parallelly, implementing their functionality. Each microservice is assigned to a specific area of an application (bounded context) and is responsible to execute its business functionalities. Developers can also add and deploy additional microservices functionalities independently without affecting other parts of the systems. Because of these characteristics, more and more enterprise applications have begun using microservices in their design.

Amazon Web Services has changed the dynamics of hosting modern applications with the introduction of a serverless application called Lambda. Initially, Lambda was used to perform small tasks like forwarding messages, transform messages, raising events, published messages. However, with the advancement of Lambda, it is now fully capable of hosting large enterprise-level backend applications without much effort. Developers don't need to care about servers, scaling, and resiliency, which are handled by AWS serverless platform. Many developers also host their microservices on Kubernetes and are supposed to be cloud-agnostic. Ideally, developers can host their Kubernetes application in any cloud provider. However, it is not as easy as it seems because each cloud vendor has a different SaaS for hosting the Kubernetes application with its configurations. Also, Kubernetes has its learning path and as your application grows, you must maintain all the infrastructure-related software used in the Kubernetes cluster. In Lambda, you don't have to maintain anything related to infrastructure (but your code). However, you will be attached to AWS cloud if you start using Lambda for your application, as no other cloud provider serverless platform is as mature as AWS. Recently, AWS has also introduced a new feature in Lambda where now you can host your containers directly in Lambda, but it is not covered in this book.

The primary goal of this book is to provide information and skills that are necessary to understand, build, and host AWS serverless applications in your environment. This book contains some practical examples to show you how to install, configure, and manage serverless applications, as well as how to communicate with different microservices and monitor and automate deployment. Over the 11 chapters in this book, you will learn the following:

Chapter 1 introduces microservices and their characteristics. It also discusses how microservice is different from monolithic applications and the challenges faced while designing microservice.

Chapter 2 discusses the concepts of ASP.NET Core Web API hosting strategy and serverless application components.

Chapter 3 discusses Amazon Web Services concepts and its services mainly used to host microservices.

Chapter 4 describes microservices patterns to follow while designing it to make it performant, resilient, and loosely coupled.

Chapter 5 discusses where we start building microservice and configure different AWS services for hosting.

Chapter 6 describes how microservices communication patterns introduce event-driven architecture and service discovery.

Chapter 7 shows the practical implementation of microservice communication and AWS services involved while implementing it.

Chapter 8 describes the monitoring tools used for microservices design.

Chapter 9 introduces Lambda authorizer and AWS Cognito to provide security to microservices.

Chapter 10 introduces AWS CodeBuild and AWS CodeDeploy for serverless application CI/CD pipeline.

Chapter 11 discusses some of the best practices to follow while implementing serverless applications in real-time projects.

Downloading the code bundle and coloured images:

Please follow the link to download the
Code Bundle and the *Coloured Images* of the book:

https://rebrand.ly/8c6d77

Errata

We take immense pride in our work at BPB Publications and follow best practices to ensure the accuracy of our content to provide with an indulging reading experience to our subscribers. Our readers are our mirrors, and we use their inputs to reflect and improve upon human errors, if any, that may have occurred during the publishing processes involved. To let us maintain the quality and help us reach out to any readers who might be having difficulties due to any unforeseen errors, please write to us at :

errata@bpbonline.com

Your support, suggestions and feedbacks are highly appreciated by the BPB Publications' Family.

Did you know that BPB offers eBook versions of every book published, with PDF and ePub files available? You can upgrade to the eBook version at www.bpbonline.com and as a print book customer, you are entitled to a discount on the eBook copy. Get in touch with us at :

business@bpbonline.com for more details.

At **www.bpbonline.com**, you can also read a collection of free technical articles, sign up for a range of free newsletters, and receive exclusive discounts and offers on BPB books and eBooks.

BPB is searching for authors like you

If you're interested in becoming an author for BPB, please visit **www.bpbonline.com** and apply today. We have worked with thousands of developers and tech professionals, just like you, to help them share their insight with the global tech community. You can make a general application, apply for a specific hot topic that we are recruiting an author for, or submit your own idea.

The code bundle for the book is also hosted on GitHub at **https://github. com/bpbpublications/Building-Modern-Serverless-Web-APIs**. In case there's an update to the code, it will be updated on the existing GitHub repository.

We also have other code bundles from our rich catalog of books and videos available at **https://github.com/bpbpublications**. Check them out!

PIRACY

If you come across any illegal copies of our works in any form on the internet, we would be grateful if you would provide us with the location address or website name. Please contact us at **business@bpbonline.com** with a link to the material.

If you are interested in becoming an author

If there is a topic that you have expertise in, and you are interested in either writing or contributing to a book, please visit **www.bpbonline.com**.

REVIEWS

Please leave a review. Once you have read and used this book, why not leave a review on the site that you purchased it from? Potential readers can then see and use your unbiased opinion to make purchase decisions, we at BPB can understand what you think about our products, and our authors can see your feedback on their book. Thank you!

For more information about BPB, please visit **www.bpbonline.com**.

Table of Contents

CHAPTER 1

Microservices – Its Characteristics and Challenges

> A microservice architectural style is an approach to develop a single application as a suite of small services, each running in its process and communicating with lightweight mechanisms, often an HTTP resource API.
>
> *-- James Lewis and Martin Fowler (2014)*

Introduction

Software developers are in a constant scuffle to find how changes related to one functionality should not affect other functionalities of a system and how to test these changes. Since the business requirements are often independent of each other, the software which we will build should also work in the same way. Most of the legacy applications are monolithic, where all the functionalities are in one place that becomes a **Big Ball of Mud (BBoM)**. -The Big Ball of Mud is a *spaghetti-code* jungle, duct-taped with slight functionality changes to these systems need regression testing to confirm other functionalities are intact. These applications require significant downtime for deployment affecting business operations and processes. Monolithic applications are hard to maintain and because of the complex deployment life cycle, many companies and developers are moving towards the microservice architecture to overcome these problems.

Structure

In this chapter, we will discuss the following topics:

- What are microservices
- Challenges
- Characteristics
- Introduction to domain-driven design

Objective

In this chapter, you will study the background of microservices, their characteristics, and challenges. If you are new to microservices, this chapter will provide you enough information to understand the subsequent chapters of this book.

Towards the end of this chapter, you will have a good idea about microservices, how it differs from monolithic applications, and why we should use it.

An introduction to Microservices

A microservice application is a collection of independent services that can scale, test, and deploy independently. Some characteristics of microservices are loosely coupled, language-independent, and self-deployable. With this architecture, different teams can work on independent unique solutions using their favorite programming language.

Let us understand microservice architecture with an example. Suppose your company put up a requirement for a basic ordering system.

Firstly, we will see how monolithic architecture looks like in this scenario. In **monolithic applications,** the user interface, business layer, and data access layer are all grouped together. All business functionalities like validation, processing orders, and sending notifications are grouped in a single code base, making it difficult to change. Changes to one business functionality might affect other functionalities of the system.

In the following monolithic layered architecture diagram, all the layers are clubbed into a single process and communicate to a single database. If anyone part of the system stops responding, the entire system will come down.

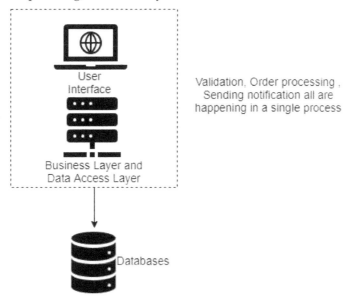

Figure 1.1: Monolithic Application

Now, with the help of microservice architecture, we have divided the monolithic application into different microservices based on different business functionalities. Since each service is independent of the other in terms of business and storage, they can achieve resiliency. Changes in one service don't require the downtime of the whole application and can deploy independently.

The following diagram shows a scenario where the microservices are in action when a user places an order from a portal. The first customer microservice validates the customer information. Once successful, the processor microservice processes the order. Finally, the response sends back to the customer the order status using the notification microservice. These microservices run autonomously and do the specific tasks assigned to them, honoring the separation of the concerns design principle. These services are loosely coupled and not dependent on each other. The order microservice doesn't know what customer microservice is doing. All the microservices are communicating with each other using the event bus. The event bus works on a publish-subscribe pattern, where the microservice publishes the events, and all the other microservices listen to the events and can subscribe to them.

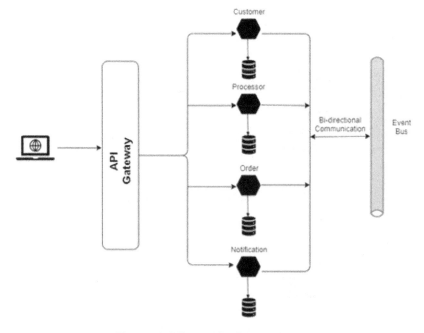

Figure 1.2: *Microservice Communication*

Note: In this book, we will illustrate Microservices by ⬢ which denote Microservice and ⬚ show its respective database to persist data.

We can also take an example of our body parts (application) divided into microservices. The function of the heart is to pump blood, lungs to respirate, kidneys to filter water (single responsibility). Each of the body parts is doing its function and is independent of each other (loosely coupled). However, they need to work in synchronization to make the system work. In case there is some issue with the heart, it will not affect the lungs. We can have a treatment discretely for the heart, and resolve the issue (independent deployment).

Characteristics of Microservices

In this section, we will discuss few characteristics of Microservices that made them attractive to use in modern applications:

- **Stateless**: Microservices are stateless and handle each request independently, without considering previous responses.

- **Decentralized database**: Each microservice has its own database as shown in the following diagram, which is used to segregate the persistence logic. This also provides an opportunity, especially in the cloud, where you can increase/decrease the database instance size as per its load.

The following diagram shows each microservice has its own persistence resource.

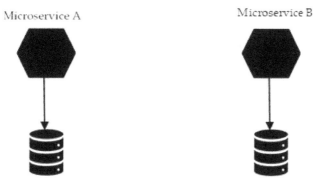

Figure 1.3: *Distributed Databases*

Note: In AWS, we have different database instance sizes based on family, memory, and CPU size. For example, db.t3.large instance is under the t3 family which has 2 vCPU (virtual CPU)/8 GB memory, and db.r5.large is under the r5 family which has 2 vCPU/16 GB memory. The database provisioning cost increases as the instance size increases. So, you need to decide which family and size are ideal for your application.

- **Language agnostic**: Another advantage of microservices is that they do not bound it to one programming language. Two teams can work in different microservices in altogether different programming languages like C#, Java, and Ruby.

- **Expose business functionality**: Microservices can expose their business functionality through API. They can implement the open API specification using swagger such that if other teams want to consume some of its functionalities, they will know the request/response format by referring to the swagger endpoints.

- **Autonomous deployment**: Since microservices are independent of each other and have a distributed database, they can deploy independently with no dependencies.

- **Elastic**: Microservices can scale out and scale in according to the load. Scale-out means adding the resources, and scale-in means removing the resources horizontally as per need. Since microservices are stateless, they will not have any effect on response.

The following diagram shows how microservices react to load by scale in and scale out.

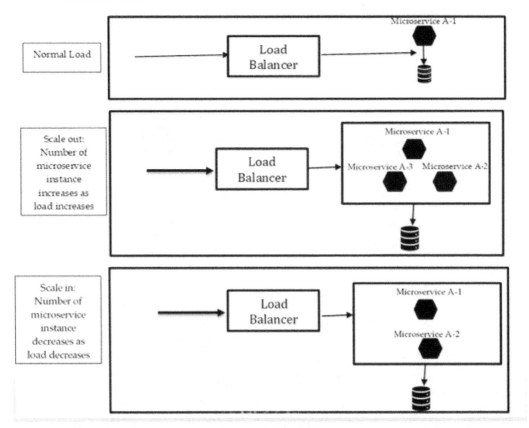

Figure 1.4: Elasticity

Note : Horizontal scaling means adding more instances to the existing pool of resources and Vertical scaling means increase CPU/memory size to the existing resources.

- **Resilient**: One characteristic which makes microservice striking is its resiliency. Microservices fail in silos and will not have any effect on the entire system. The developers can work on that Microservice and deploy it independently to resolve their issues. Because of its resiliency, the microservice system has minimum downtime at the time of service failure.

The following diagram shows microservice application resiliency. Even if one microservice failed the application is still up and running.

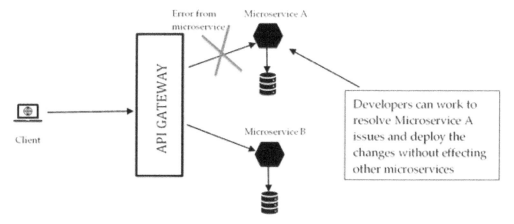

Figure 1.5: Microservice resiliency

- **CI/CD**: The ease of doing **Continuous Integration/Continuous Deployment** is another characteristic of microservices. Each Microservice can deploy by configuring its own build and release pipeline. The developers can configure their build pipeline to start when the code merges into the master branch. The build pipeline will start building the solution, run respective test cases, run custom scripts, and generate artifacts to a build location. The release pipeline then deploys those build artifacts.

The following diagram shows the step involved deploying microservice to cloud using CI/CD pipeline.

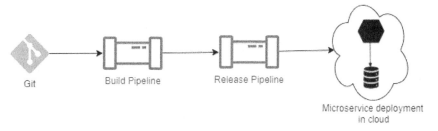

Figure 1.6: Microservice CI/CD pipeline

Challenges

Because of the loosely coupled nature and distributed database of microservices, there are challenges while we design microservices. Here, we will discuss the challenges that we usually face while designing microservices. In this book, we will discuss the patterns on how to resolve a few of these challenges:

- **Resources**: The number of resources is directly proportional to the number of microservices. As the number of microservice increases, the number of resources also increases. Sometimes, it is difficult to maintain and monitor an overwhelming number of resources.

- **Complex distributed monitoring and logging**: The distributed nature of microservices makes it hard to monitor and analyse. In AWS, the CloudWatch is used for monitoring, collecting logs, and analysing.

- **Complex tracing:** Tracing is another important aspect of a microservices application. Tracing is used to track the request flow in your application which is useful to identify the service in case of failure. AWS X-Ray service is used for distributed tracing.

- **Brownfield applications**: A developer can design and develop microservice by following good practices in case of an application where the client is developing the system from scratch. However, in most of the scenarios, developers deal with the brownfield applications like converting monolithic to microservice. This becomes difficult because usually, in monolithic, everything is tied up to a single database, and segregating into multiple services with a single database becomes a challenge. The Domain Driven Design (DDD) principles and strangler patterns can be used to segregate the brownfield applications to microservices.

- **Polyglot**: Sometimes, the polyglot approach leads to unmaintainable service. For example, a team develops one microservice in a language that the other teams don't know. Usually, they restrain from changing those microservices, which lead to service zombies.

- **Distributed database**: This has raised new challenges concerning data consistency. Microservices usually follow the eventual consistency model for high availability, which guarantees that the data that comes to one replica will eventually be updated to all the other replicas. Since the distributed database architecture cannot leverage the **Atomicity, Consistency, Integration, and Durable (ACID)** transactions, we end up using the partial transactions. in case of failure, we need to accurately roll back from all the affected services to overcome the data inconsistency.

- **DevOps complexity**: The use of multiple technologies and synchronize deployment is challenging.

- **Security**: It becomes a challenge to maintain security for each of the distributed and autonomous microservice. For microservices, a centralized security system is ideal for developers.

- **Testing**: Integration testing is another challenge for microservices. If 100 microservices communicate with each other, it makes the integration testing hell.

Domain-Driven Design (DDD)

In this section, you will get a brief introduction to the **domain-driven design** (DDD) and how it is used to internally segregate the microservice responsibility.

DDD is a design principle that can be applied while designing the microservice. The DDD is a set of patterns and practices which assist us to come up with a neat solution and rich domain model. In the DDD, a proper distillation of enormous problems into sub-problem exposes the core functionalities, which is of utmost importance for the business. Understanding the DDD technical rules and patterns require steep learning. The bounded context plays a significant role in the DDD to determine the boundaries and responsibilities of a microservice. Two rules follow while we deal with the bounded context: cohesion and coupling. You should build a boundary around the parts that need cohesion and don't divide the microservice into tiny functionalities to avoid chattiness.

The DDD divides the applications into layers. Most enterprise application divides its business and technical complexities into layers. Layers are the logical segregation of code and help manage the complexity of the code. These layers depend on each other through the **dependency injection** (DI). Let us now discuss layers:

- **Domain layer**: This layer contains the core business functionalities. All the shared packages and complex business rules come under the domain layer. The domain layer deals with entities, value objects, and aggregators to design complex applications.

- **Application layer**: This layer provides the functionality to interact with UI. The UI will communicate with the application layer using a communication channel, like the REST endpoint. This layer depends on the domain layer for the entity object and the infrastructure layer for the repository object.

- **Infrastructure layer**: This layer handles all the tasks related to the infrastructure like a database. This layer will deal with all the operations related to the infrastructure. It depends on the domain layer for entity mapping.

Tip: Try to apply the DDD while dealing with complex microservices. Simple approaches can manage simple microservices

NOTE: The dependency injection is a pattern used to inject object dependencies on the fly rather than create them. We will discuss the DI elaborately in the upcoming chapters.

The following diagram shows interaction between DDD Layers.

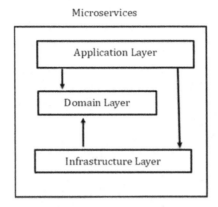

Figure 1.7: *DDD layers*

Ideally, the domain layer should not depend on any other layers. In the future, if a company wants to migrate or use its business logic into some other application, it can migrate the domain layer without changing any business rules.

Conclusion

Developers have used microservices for decades on modern applications. However, there are still some challenges that need proper designing, discussion, and understanding of the business rules. A too small or too big Microservice can affect the performance of your application significantly. So, follow some of the best practices while designing your microservices to gain significant performance. In the next chapter, we will see more on different aspects of Microservices and the tools available in AWS.

Points to Remember

- The Big Ball of Mud is a haphazardly structured, sprawling, sloppy, duct-tape-and-baling-wire, **spaghetti-code** jungle and slight functionality changes to these systems need regression testing to confirm other functionalities are intact.

- A microservice application is a collection of independent services that can be scaled, tested, and deployed independently.

- Microservices are stateless and don't depend on the previous response.

- Some of the characteristics of microservices are loose coupling, language-agnostic, resilient, and autonomous deployment.

- A software design pattern solves a commonly occurring problem in a software design.

- A domain driven design is a set of principles, patterns, and practices used to design complex microservices.

- In a DDD, the domain layer comprises the core functionalities of an application.

Key Terms

- **Microservice**: It is a collection of independent services that can scale, test, and deploy independently

- **Monolithic**: Single application multiple modules tightly coupled with each other.

- **Dependency injection**: This is a pattern used to inject object dependencies on the fly rather than creating them.

- **Domain-driven design**: This is a set of principles, patterns, and practices used to design complex microservices.

Questions

1. What are microservices?

2. List a few characteristics of microservices?

3. How do microservice applications differ from monolithic applications?

4. What is the difference between horizontal and vertical scaling?

5. List a few challenges faced while designing microservices?

6. What are the DDD principles and their layers?

7. What is the responsibility of the domain layer?

8. What are the entities in a DDD?

9. What is a DI (dependency injection) and its types?

10. How does the DI make an application loosely coupled?

Multiple choice questions

1. **Does a monolithic architecture adhere to a loosely couple design?**

   a) True

   b) False

2. **Which of the following are not Microservice characteristics?**

   a) Loosely coupled

   b) Single responsibility

   c) Stateful

   d) None of these

3. **Microservices has a complex monitoring process.**

   a) True

   b) False

4. **In the DDD, the domain layer should be independent of other layers.**

   a) True

   b) False

5. **Which of the following is not a microservice challenge?**

   a) Brownfield application

   b) Polyglot approach

   c) Resiliency

   d) None of the above

Answer

1. b
2. c
3. a
4. a
5. c

CHAPTER 2

Introduction to ASP.NET Core Web API

> **ASP.NET Core** is a cross-platform, high-performance, and *open-source* framework for building modern, cloud-enabled, Internet-connected apps.
>
> *--- Microsoft*

Introduction

With the introduction of .NET Core, a whole new world for .NET developers has opened who can now run their code on Linux and macOS besides Windows. ASP.NET Core is a cross-platform, free, and open-source software developed by the Microsoft community. Today, major cloud providers like AWS, Google, and Azure support .NET Core and allow developers to build/deploy the application seamlessly on their cloud environments. Earlier, the .NET framework ran only on Windows machines and didn't support the cross-platform functionality. However, with the development of .NET Core, Microsoft has recommended using it for high performance, scalability, modularity, and cross-platform applications.

Some features that make .NET Core attractive to build modern applications are as follows:

- **Modular architecture**: Modular architecture means you don't need to install all the packages irrespective of their uses. Install packages only what you need using a NuGet repository. The architecture is modularized using the NuGet packages where every assembly is packed and shipped as a NuGet package.

- **Supports a variety of system architectures**: It supports a wide variety of devices, ranging from the Raspberry Pi to docker containers. You can build an application on your system, and move the code using the lift and shift approach.

- **Command-line tools**: The .NET Core command-line interface supports a wide variety of commands, like new, build, publish, etc. You can create your own shared utility package using the NuGet command and publish it in the private or public repository.

> **Note: Lift and shift is an approach where you can migrate your application to any environment (from on-premises to cloud) as it is.**
>
> **A NuGet package is a single ZIP file with a .nupkg extension that contains the compiled code Dynamic Link Libraries (DLLs), other files related to that code, and a descriptive manifest that includes information like the package's version number.**

Structure

In this chapter, we will discuss the following topics:

- Anatomy of ASP.NET Core Web API
  - o Hosting strategy
  - o REST services
  - o Controllers
  - o OpenAPI/Swagger

- Installation and configuration
  - o AWS ToolKit

- Different components of the serverless project
  - o Lambda entry points
  - o Profile
  - o Deployment

Objectives

If you are new to ASP.NET Core, it is recommended that you gather its basic knowledge and then start this chapter for better understanding. This chapter will not cover the basics of ASP.NET Core. In this chapter, we will learn only those concepts of ASP.NET Core which are required to understand the subsequent chapters of this book.

You will be introduced to the AWS serverless application and the tools needed to build it.

Towards the end of this chapter, you will have a good idea about the AWS serverless application, its components, and the REST API.

After completing this chapter, you will be able to understand ASP.NET Core concepts, ASP.NET Core hosting strategy, and the anatomy of ASP.NET Core Web API.

In this section, we will discuss some important parts of ASP.NET Core Web API for a better understanding of its functionalities.

Hosting strategy

As we already know, ASP.NET Core applications are the console applications that use an inbuilt Kestrel webserver to handle the request. Kestrel is an open-source, lightweight, cross-platform web server that is high in performance. It can expose an edge server or provision behind the proxy server.

- With an edge server, Kestrel is directly exposed to the internet, and it serves all the incoming requests.

The following diagram illustrates the Kestrel web server's direct interaction with the internet.

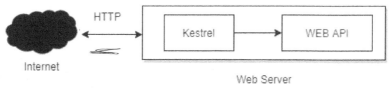

Figure 2.1: Kestrel as Edge Server

However, it is not recommended by the Microsoft community as it does not support the host headers. This means it will only host one web server listening on one port. It also doesn't support HTTP->HTTPS that is, the SSL redirection, which can eventually hurt the security of your web API application. Microsoft recommends putting Kestrel behind a web server that acts as a reverse proxy, like IIS and Apache, to increase security and performance. These servers intercept requests to Kestrel that eventually forward the request to the ASP.NET Core web application.

The following diagram illustrates Kestrel's interaction with the internet through a reverse proxy:

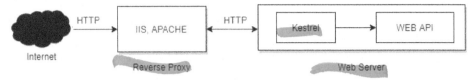

Figure 2.2: *Kestrel behind a proxy server*

Now, the question that might arise is why use Kestrel when the IIS server is already being used to host web servers for so many years. The answer is because the IIS server supports only Windows OS. Also, to support the cross-platform functionality, ASP.NET Core needs to support different web servers, which eventually becomes hard to maintain. To resolve this issue, Microsoft introduced Kestrel, which runs behind these servers seamlessly without bothering about hosting the environment.

Running the IIS and Apache as reverse proxy servers have the following advantages to improve the performance of your application:

- **Load balancing**: The reverse proxy server routes the incoming HTTP requests to several identical web servers.

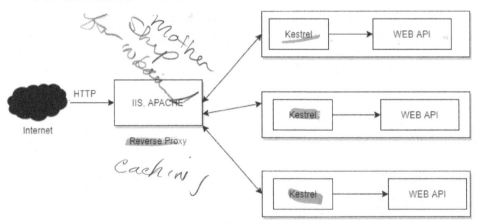

Figure 2.3: *Reverse Proxy Load Balancing*

- **Security**: An added extra layer of defense for authentication.

- **Caching**: The reverse proxy can also cache the data which reduces the load to a back-end server.

- **Compression**: Compresses the data to reduce latency.

- **SSL**: Handles incoming SSL connection request, decrypts the data, and passes it to the web servers. It removes the need to install an SSL certificate for each underlying web server.

A reverse proxy is a server that intercepts requests from the internet and forwards them to the underlying web server. It intercepts requests from clients to servers. It is recommended that you do not expose the Kestrel web server directly to the outside world because of security. However, with the introduction of reverse proxy, it will add an extra hop to the request/response.

REST services

REST stands for Representational State Transfer and it was first introduced by Roy Fielding in 2000. REST is an architectural style used to connect networked systems through HTTP in a loosely coupled fashion. In the REST Web Services, the endpoints are represented by **a Uniform Resource Identifier** (**URI**) which provides resource representation, such as JSON and HTTP methods. Each URI should unambiguously identify the resources within a system. The following are the basic HTTP methods used with status code:

Method	Description	Success Status Code
GET	Return a resource	200
POST	Add a new resource	201
PUT	Update a new resource	204
DELETE	Delete a resource	204

Table 2.1: *List of the REST HTTP Verbs*

There is no hard-and-fast rule to use a specific status code for specific methods. You can use 200 status codes to represent success for PUT and DELETE based on your design. However, using the standard status code helps readability and maintainability.

Some of the benefits of the **Restful services** are that they are lightweight, stateless, scalable, support open API specification, and easy-to-implement. Most of the modern applications use REST in the ASP.NET Core project to build microservices. However, one significant disadvantage of REST is the response **payload size**. You cannot ask the server to return only those specific fields that are required and not all the fields in the payload.

Controllers

The ASP.NET Core application uses a controller to handle the REST messages. It exposes an endpoint to the outside world to interact with the application. In ASP. NET Core, Web API, the controllers are derived from the **ControllerBase** class and not from the **Controller** class. Eventually, the **Controller** class derives from

ControllerBase and adds support for views that are not needed in the Web API application.

The following code represents a simple **Controller** derives from **ControllerBase** class.

```
1.      [Route("api/[controller]")]
2.      public class ValuesController : ControllerBase
3.      {
4.          // GET api/values
5.          [HttpGet]
6.          public IEnumerable<string> Get()
7.          {
8.              return new string[] { "value1", "value2" };
9.          }
10.
11.         // GET api/values/5
12.         [HttpGet("{id}")]
13.         public IActionResult Get(int id)
14.         {
15.             if (id == 0)
16.                 return NotFound();
17.             else
18.                 return Ok();
19.         }
20.     }
```

In the preceding code, the **ValueController** class is derived from the **ControllerBase** class and exposes two GET methods as indicated by the attribute [**HttpGet**]. The return type of the method can be a primitive or complex type, which returns only one type of data. In the case of the first GET method, collection of strings are returned. In the second GET method, the response changes based on the Id value. The route attribute "**api/[controller]**" defines **api/nameofthecontroller**. Here, the name of the controller is Value. Whenever you create a controller in ASP. NET Core, it will append the controller with the name. So, now when you run this application, Kestrel will host this web application locally and assign a port number. To call the first method, use **http://localhost:4000/api/values** and for the second method, use **http://localhost:4000/api/values/5**. The URL's endpoint should be unique to identify which method needs to be invoked.

> **Note: Postman is a free testing tool used by professionals to test the REST Web API.**

OpenAPI/Swagger

OpenAPI/Swagger is a language-agonistic specification to define the REST API which reduces the development effort by generating efficient documentation. While consuming endpoints, the developers refer to the OpenAPI documentation to understand the request/response payload models and the status code. It helps them to understand the capabilities of the disassociating services without access to the implementation.

The following screenshot illustrates the swagger UI when you run the swagger configured ASP.NET Core application:

Figure 2.4: Swagger endpoint details

In this book, we will use the **Swashbuckle.AspNetCore** NuGet package is an open-source project to generate the OpenAPI documentation for the ASP.NET Core API.

> **Note: OpenAPI and Swagger are the same and can be used interchangeably; however, OpenAPI is preferred.**

Installation and configuration

In this section, we will discuss the installation of Visual Studio AWS Toolkit and learn how to create ASP.NET Core Web API Lambda projects.

AWS Toolkit

In this section, we will discuss the ASP.NET Core anatomies as per the serverless Lambda project in Visual Studio 2019. To install the AWS-related template, go to **https://aws.amazon.com/visualstudio/** and download the AWS Toolkit for Visual

Studio 2017 and 2019. After installing it, we will create a new project and then select the AWS serverless application.

The following screenshot depicts Visual Studio where you can select the AWS Lambda project:

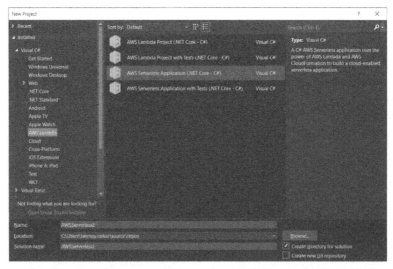

Figure 2.5: Visual Studio screenshot to select AWS Lambda project

After you select the project type, it will ask you to select the blueprints. Blueprints are the Lambda projects that contain the starter code for your functions and a test project.

The following screenshot shows the selection of the ASP.NET Core Web API blueprint from the available options:

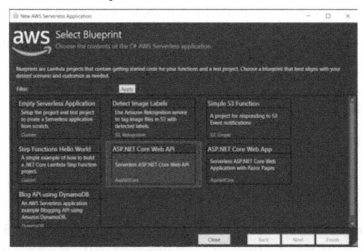

Figure 2.6: Select ASP.Net Core Web API project blueprint

Since this book explains creating and hosting serverless Web API, here we will select the **ASP.NET Core Web API** and click **Finish**.

Once you click **Finish**, the Lambda project will get created with a few sample controllers and configuration files.

The following screenshot shows the ASP.NET Core Web API serverless application project structure:

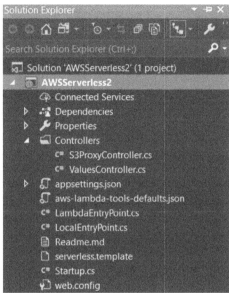

Figure 2.7: Serverless application project structure

Under the controller folder, two files namely S3ProxyController and ValueController will get created. The ValueController contains a simple REST HTTP endpoint structure. The S3ProxyController has endpoints to list, update, or delete the S3 objects from the S3 buckets. The name of the S3 bucket comes from the **AppS3Bucket** key in the **appsettings.json** file.

Different components of the serverless project

In this section, we will discuss some of the generated Lambda project files and their significance.

Lambda entry points

There are two entry files in the serverless project namely **LambdaEntryPoint** and **LocalEntryPoint**. When you run the application locally, ASP.NET Core considers the LocalEntryPoint configuration as an entry point. As we know that ASP.NET Core is a console application, you can see the main method where the execution started. Under the main method, **BuildWebHost** will be called which will create **WebHost** with the default builder settings. The default builder uses Kestrel as a web server. Set the IHostingEvironment content path to **GetCurrentDirectory** (root folder of the application which contains the startup class and configuration files), load configuration files.

The following code represents the `LocalEntryPoint` configuration

```
public class LocalEntryPoint
1.          {
2.              public static void Main(string[] args)
3.              {
4.                  BuildWebHost(args).Run();
5.              }
6.
7.              public static IWebHost BuildWebHost(string[] args) =>
8.                  WebHost.CreateDefaultBuilder(args)
9.                      .UseStartup<Startup>()
10.                     .Build();
11.         }
```

The following image shows a typical HTTP request flow for the ASP.NET Core hosting:

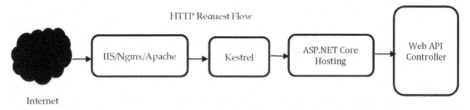

Figure 2.8: ASP.Net Core HTTP Request Flow

After the application gets deployed in the cloud, the **LambdaEntryPoint** configuration will be used as a Lambda function entry point. This is a very basic implementation where the APIGatewayProxy function is used as a base class. Here, the API gateway acts as a reverse proxy, and the Lambda function host the ASP.NET Core Web API application. The builder inside the **Init** function will configure logging, API gateway, and other configurations. The startup class needs to be configured with the custom settings.

The following code represents the LambdaEntry point configuration which is derived from APIGatewayProxyFunction.

```
    public class LambdaEntryPoint :
1.          Amazon.Lambda.AspNetCoreServer.APIGatewayProxyFunction
2.      {
3.          protected override void Init(IWebHostBuilder builder)
4.          {
5.              builder
6.                  .UseStartup<Startup>();
7.          }
8.      }
```

The following figure represents the HTTP request flow when the ASP.NET Core Web API is hosted in the AWS serverless environment:

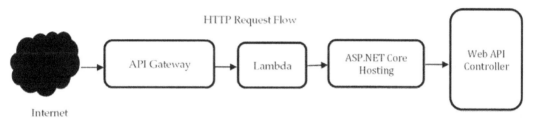

Figure 2.9: *HTTP Request Flow when ASP.Net Core hosted in AWS Serverless Environment*

Profile

When you run the application, you will get two options to choose from based on where you want to host your web server. These are the IIS Express or the Kestrel. The settings are defined as profile under **Properties | launchSettings.json**. The IIS Express settings are mentioned under the **iisSettings** section where you can change the port number and authentication. The Kestrel settings are defined under the project name.

Deployment

To deploy the webserver on AWS Lambda from the Visual Studio, you need to change the configurations, like AWS region, template, and stack name as per your settings under **AWS-lambda-tools-defaults.json**. Then, right-click and click on **Publish**.

Conclusion

In this chapter, we mostly discussed the ASP.NET Core Web API structure, its relations, and how to create a serverless project which can be hosted in the AWS Lambda. We also discussed different hosting strategies when running locally as well as on the cloud. You might have noticed that most of the heavy lifting, like scaling and hosting is taken care of by the AWS Lambda which allows the developers to focus more on the design and code rather than the infrastructure. In the upcoming chapters, we will understand how AWS provisions different resources on the cloud and some of the services which we will use in this book.

Points to remember

- ASP.NET Core is a cross-platform software that runs on multiple operating systems.

- Kestrel is an open-source, lightweight, cross-platform web server that is high in performance.

- A reverse proxy is a server that intercepts requests from the internet and forwards them to the underlying web server.

- REST stands for REpresentational State Transfer and is lightweight, stateless, easy-to-implement, supports OpenAPI specification, and is scalable.

- In ASP.Net Core, the Web API controllers are derived from the ControllerBase class and not from the Controller class.

- OpenAPI/Swagger is a language-agonistic specification to define the REST API which reduces the development effort by generating efficient documentation.

- When deployed to Lambda, the API gateway acts as a reverse proxy and the lambda function hosts the ASP.NET Core Web API application.

Key terms

- **ASP.NET Core**: ASP.NET Core is a cross-platform, free, open-source software developed by the Microsoft community.

- **Kestrel**: It is an open-source, lightweight, cross-platform web server that is high in performance.

- **Reverse proxy**: A reverse proxy is a server that intercepts requests from the internet and forwards them to the underlying web server.

- **REST**: REST is an architectural style to connect networked systems through HTTP in a loosely coupled fashion.

- **OpenAPI**: This is a language-agonistic specification to define the REST API which reduces the development effort by generating efficient documentation.

Multiple choice questions

1. **Which of the following is an open-source, lightweight, cross-platform web server?**
   a) IIS
   b) Kestrel
   c) None of the above

2. **Which of the following is not a characteristic of reverse proxy?**
   a) Load balancing
   b) Security
   c) Caching
   d) Hosting

3. **Which of the following is not a valid HTTP method?**
   a) GET
   b) POST
   c) REMOVE
   d) DELETE

4. **ASP.Net Core Web API controller should always be derived from which base class:**
   a) Controller
   b) ControllerBase
   c) ValueController

5. **OpenAPI specification is used to:**
   a) Generate REST API documentation
   b) Create a controller code
   c) Generate REST API project
   d) None of the above

6. **What is the role of the API gateway when the ASP.NET Core Web API is deployed in AWS Lambda?**

   a) Router

   b) Reverse proxy

   c) Switch

   d) None of the above

Answer

1. b
2. d
3. c
4. b
5. a
6. b

Chapter 3

Introduction to AWS Services

> **The cloud services companies of all sizes…The cloud is for everyone. The cloud is a democracy.**
>
> *--Marc Benioff, Founder, CEO, and Chairman of Salesforce*

Introduction

Amazon Web Services is one of the leading cloud service providers with over 100 services to choose from. It offers services like Infrastructure as a Service (IaaS), Platform as a Service (PaaS), Software as a Service (SaaS), and Function as a Service (FaaS). As of now, the AWS cloud spreads around 77 availability zones within 24 geographic regions around the world. Each availability zone contains multiple data centres. As a user, you can select and deploy your services in any of the zones in any part of the world based on your business user base. Some of the benefits that encourage so many companies to move their on-premises operations to AWS are security, availability, performance, and scalability. Since AWS has undertaken most of the heavy lifting, it allows these companies to focus more on their application design and code. In the initial days, it requires a separate team to maintain the on-premises database and application servers and maintain it for scalability and availability (mostly at the time of heavy traffic). Usually, their scaling strategy is to add more CPU and memory to exiting servers and once that gets exhausted, they add more servers to scale horizontally. On cold days when the traffic is low, most of the resources remain unutilized which eventually add up unnecessary costs to the monthly billing. Also, the companies have to maintain the database and the application server team, which further adds cost to their monthly spending. Fortunately, today with the introduction of AWS, you pay as you go. Pay only for the resources that you use. Let us suppose you have hosted your web application on the EC2 instance (virtual machine), and usually every year in May, your business expects heavy traffic. In AWS, you can create rules which scale up (by adding more EC2 instances) as the traffic increases and scale down (by removing EC2 instances) as the traffic decreases. This way, you only pay for the resources you use. This has been a huge benefit for the companies who can now maintain their resources efficiently and in a cost-effective way. With DevOps getting popular, the developers themselves maintaining the applications and database servers, further reducing the cost. In the upcoming section, we will get familiar with the AWS services that we will use in this book and some of the AWS terminology.

Structure

In this chapter, we will discuss the following topics:

- Anatomy of AWS
  - Region
  - Availability zone
  - Virtual Private Cloud
  - Network Access Control Layer
  - Subnet
  - Security group
  - Elastic Compute Cloud
  - Route table
  - Internet gateway
  - NAT gateway
  - Load balancer
  - Auto Scaling group
  - Route 53
  - API gateway
  - Lambda
  - Relational Database Service

- o   Simple Storage Service
- o   Elastic cache
- o   Monitoring
- Some important services
  - o   **Identity and Access Management (IAM)**
  - o   Parameter store
  - o   Tags
  - o   **Simple Queue Service (SQS)**
  - o   **Simple Notification Service (SNS)**
  - o   Step functions

Objective

In this chapter, you will learn the basics of AWS concepts, like regions and availability zones. You will also learn about some of the AWS services to make your application highly available, scalable, and secure which we will use in the subsequent chapters.

Towards the end of this chapter, you will have a better understanding of the AWS terminologies and the services available to build microservices.

Anatomy of AWS

In this section, we will go through the AWS terminologies and concepts required to understand the working of your application when provisioned on AWS.

The following diagram represents the architecture of the webserver hosted on EC2 instances and application API hosted on Lambda behind the API gateway. We will discuss different AWS services and their significances using this architecture.

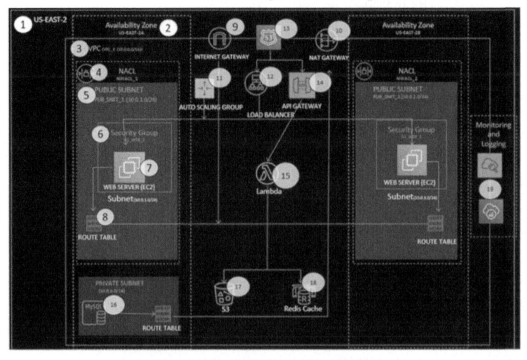

Figure 3.1: Sample AWS Architecture diagram

The numbering in the architecture diagram will help you map the number in the discussion. The direction of arrows signifies the network flow.

Region (1)

AWS operations are spread geographically and each geographical location composes of multiple regions. It isolates each region from other regions that deliver fault tolerance and high availability. When you create or view resources in AWS, it ties those resources to a region and does not automatically replicate to other regions because different regions operate under a different law of the land. However, there is an option for you to move your resources from one region to another. In India, AWS has Mumbai region (ap-south-1) with 3 availability zones (ap-south-1a, ap-south-1b, ap-south-1c).

Availability zone (2)

This segregates each region into multiple **availability zones (AZ's)**. AZ's are the data centres where your resources get hosted. You can distribute your instance into multiple AZ's to achieve fault tolerance and high availability. If for some reason, one AZ fails, there still is another AZ to process incoming requests. There are few services, like S3, which provide high availability by automatically replicating your resources to multiple AZ's.

Virtual Private Cloud (3)

Virtual Private Clouds (VPC) are software-defined networks that allow you to host your AWS resources in a logically isolated section of AWS and have full control over the network configurations. The VPC spans across multiple AZ's. You host your applications inside VPC either in a public subnet (access to the internet) or a private subnet (no access to the internet). You can also extend your corporate data centre to the AWS cloud data center using a hardware **Virtual Private Network** (**VPN**).

The following diagram shows an AWS region with multiple AZ's. The VPC spans around the multiple availability zones.

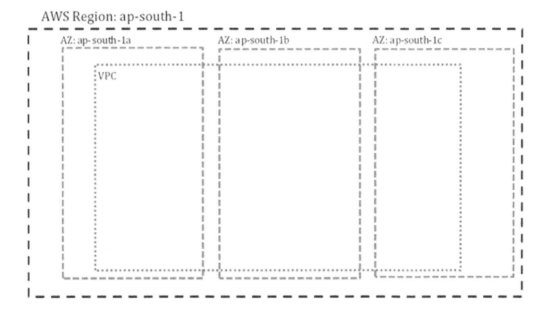

Figure 3.2: Region with multiple AZ's and VPC

Network Access Control Layer (4)

Network Access Control Layer (NACL) is a security layer for a subnet that acts as a firewall and allows communication-based on inbound and outbound rules. Whenever you create a new NACL, it will deny all communications by default. You must manually add rules to allow the specific network traffic. AWS recommends adding rule numbers in multiples of 100.

Subnet (5)

Subnets are a subset of VPC and each subnet is associate with one AZ. A subnet can be public or private. A public subnet allows the underlying resources to communicate to the internet. A private subnet restricts the incoming requests from the internet. When you want to run web servers in an EC2 instance, you need to provision that instance inside a public subnet to access it publicly. However, when you host a database server, it's better to host it under a private subnet to protect your business data from the outside world. Each subnet must have a distinct **Classless Inter-Domain Routing (CIDR)** range which is a set of IP standards used to create a unique identifier for the resources. When any resource is hosted in that subnet, it will get a unique IP address to identify that resource within your VPC. Let us suppose your VPC has a CIDR range of 10.0.0.0/16. Then, you can choose 10.0.1.0/24 and 10.0.2.0/24 CIDR for two of its subnets, respectively. Please note that AWS doesn't allow subnet masking of 8 i.e. 10.0.1.0/8 for internal use. The largest subnet IP range you can create is 10.0.1.0/16.

By default, whenever you create a subnet, it is a private subnet. To make it public, you need to attach the internet gateway to its route table.

> **Note: AWS assigns a dynamic public address to the EC2 instance and will change every time you stop or restart the instances. Often IP address change leads to network interruption. To resolve this issue, you can assign a static Elastic IP address to your resource, and once assigned to the EC2 instance, it will not change on stop or restart. However, if you terminate the instance and launch a new instance, attach the same elastic IP to the newly launched instance to resume the operation. Also, make sure that the CIDR range you choose for subnets does not overlap with each other.**

The following diagram shows that the subnet is a part of VPC and each subnet spans around only one availability zone. It also shows that NACL is a part of the subnet:

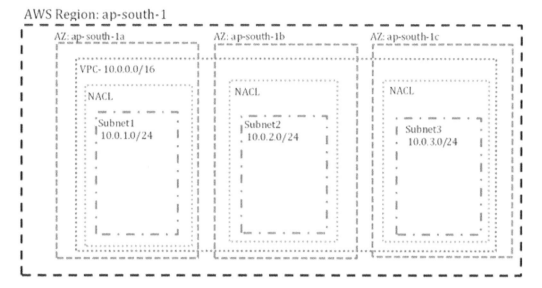

Figure 3.3: *Subnet and NACL*

Security groups (6)

The security group acts as a virtual firewall for the EC2 instances to control the incoming and outgoing traffic. You can attach one or more security groups to these instances. The security group inbound rules control the incoming traffic and the outbound rules control the outgoing traffic. AWS will evaluate each security group attached to an instance before deciding whether the traffic is allowed or not. AWS EC2 will use the default security group in case no security group is specified. You can modify the security group anytime and the changes are applied to the instance immediately.

The following diagram shows that security groups are part of the subnet and provide security to the underlying resources:

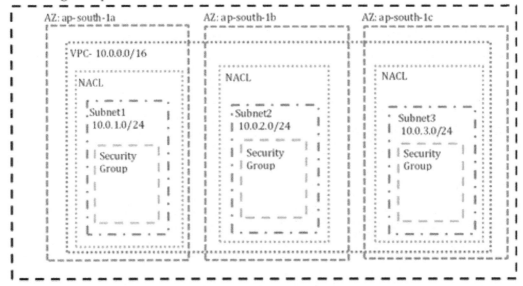

Figure 3.4: Security Groups

Elastic Compute Cloud (7)

EC2 is a web-based service that allows a business to run its application on AWS. It allows the developers to run virtual machines known as EC2 instances (consists of specific hardware and operating system) which provide compute capacity to host their application. EC2 service is one of the building blocks services of AWS. This is the most widely used service within AWS and a lot of other services depend on this service. EC2 provides a lot of benefits as follows:

- Auto Scaling
- Elasticity
- Pay-as-you-go
- Reliability
- Fault tolerance

There is a distinct class of EC2 instances with unique configurations you can choose from based on your business requirements, each having its benefit:

- General purpose
- Compute optimized
- Memory optimized

- Storage optimized

There is a different type of pricing model available as follows:

- **On-Demand Instances**: On-Demand Instances follow the pay-as-you-go pricing option. There is no long-term commitment and pay only for the time your On-Demand Instances run. You can stop, terminate, or resume anytime as needed. This is the default option when you provision a new EC2 instance.

- **Reserved Instances**: **Reserved Instances (RI)** are the instances you purchase for an availability zone within a region for a significant period (1-3 year term). RI provides a discount of up to 72% compared to On-Demand Instances.

- **Spot Instances**: Spot Instances are another purchasing option where customers can purchase unused EC2 instances at a highly reduced rate (up to 90% as compared to On-Demand Instances). These instances are acquired using the bidding process where customers bid for the price that they are willing to pay. When the EC2 instance is available at that price, the instance is provisioned for the customer. However, the caveat in this option is as soon as the market price becomes more than the customer's bidding price, AWS can terminate the instance within 2 min warning. So, go for this option only when it doesn't matter if your applications, like CI/CD, web server, test / development environment stop in between.

The following diagram shows the EC2 instances, that is, T2 instances are provisioned inside the subnet and the security group acts as a firewall:

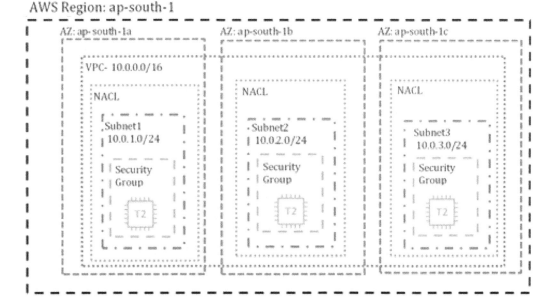

Figure 3.5: *EC2 Instance*

Route Table (8)

Each VPC has an implicit router that will direct the traffic based on the routing table. It also associates the subnets with a routing table that controls the routing for the subnet. You can create a custom route table for your subnet, and if no routing table is specified, then the subnet will be implicitly associated with the main route table. A subnet can have only one route table, but the same route table can associate with multiple subnets. Each route in a routing table has a destination and target.

Internet Gateway (9)

An internet gateway is a horizontally scaled, highly available component that allows VPC to connect to the outside world. Internet gateways are attached to VPC and it allows the internet routable traffic through VPC route tables. Also, the internet gateway performs **Network Address Translation (NAT)** for the public IP address assigned instances.

> Note: By default, when you create a subnet, it is a private subnet. To make it public, you need to attach an Internet Gateway (IG) to its route table. AWS assigns a public address to EC2 instances from its pool of IP addresses and uses Network Address Translation (NAT) to map public address to its internal private address.

NAT Gateway (10)

Network Address Translation gateway is used to enable instances inside the private subnet to communicate with the internet but not vice-versa. NAT gateway restricts the internet to initiate communication with private subnet resources. As we already discussed, private subnets are the subnets that don't have internet access and you cannot communicate with these resources from the outside world. However, the resources still need regular updates from the internet and NAT initiates a connection from these resources to the internet.

Auto Scaling Group (11)

One of the most important features of AWS is elasticity. Elasticity means you can add or remove instances as per need and pay only for the instances that are being used. The Auto Scaling group helps you achieve elasticity. It helps you to maintain the application's high availability (by automatically adding/removing instances according to the rules you define), fault tolerance, and lower costs. Auto Scaling groups help to scale up or scale down based on either the average CPU utilization, average network in, average network out, or application load balancer request count.

The Auto Scaling group has a launch template associate with it. In the Launch template, you can define **Amazon Machine Image** (**AMI**) to use instance type, storage volumes, network settings, security groups, and user script to execute at the time a new instance gets launched.

> **Note: AMI is an image/template having all the software preinstalled, like operating systems, applications, and web servers. You can either select AMI according to your application need from the AWS market or you can also create your custom AMI and use it to launch instances. Auto Scaling uses custom AMI to the provision of a new EC2 instance as needed.**

Load Balancer (12)

A load balancer distributes the incoming requests (based on a Round Robin algorithm) to its registered instances (in the target group) in one or more availability zones. Load balancer supports both the HTTP and HTTPS traffic. Load balancers are associated with the target groups where you can register your qualified instances. Once you map a load balancer to Auto Scaling, it enhances high availability and fault tolerance. If one instance gets corrupted or becomes unhealthy, the load balancer will stop the traffic to that instance. Auto Scaling service will eventually terminate that instance and initiate a new one.

The following diagram shows how the load balancer distributes traffic to instances in the Auto Scaling group. The number of instances can be added or removed based on the load:

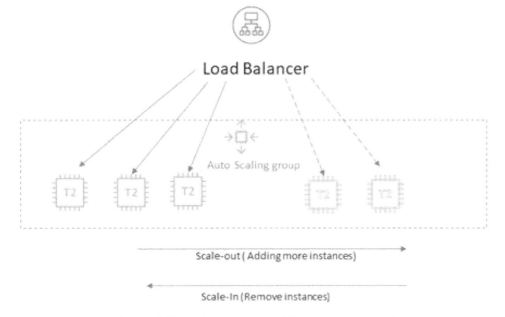

Figure 3.6: *Network flow using Load Balance and Autoscaling*

Route 53 (13)

As per AWS, Route 53 is a highly scalable and highly available Domain Name System web service. Route 53 domain registration process is quite fast and simple. It is also cost-effective, secure, and is designed to integrate with AWS services seamlessly. To host your domain in Route 53, you first need to create a hosted zone. After the successful creation of the hosted zone, you need to observe pre-populated records in your hosted zone. Then, you need to map the NS record (Name Server) to your domain hosting site (domain propagation will take some time). After that, you can specify the routing policy. There is a different routing option available as follows:

- **Simple routing**: Routing traffic to just one resource.

- **Weighted**: When two or more resources are doing the same job, you can specify the percentage of traffic that routes to each resource.

- **Geolocation**: Route traffic based on the location of the user.

- **Latency**: Route traffic to the region having the minimum latency.

- **Failover**: Route traffic to fall over a resource when the original resource was unhealthy.

- **Multivalued**: Route 53 responds to the DNS queries with up to eight healthy records selected at random.

> **Note: A Domain Name System (DNS) translates a human-readable address to an IP address. For example, it converts www.helloworld.com to 192.168.0.1.**

API Gateway (14)

API gateway is a managed service where you have configured both stateful (WebSocket) and stateless (REST and HTTP) services. API gateway handles security, monitoring, tracking, authentication, caching, and connects to your hosted backend services. The AWS gateway acts as a reverse proxy to control and distribute incoming and outgoing network traffic. You can create a stage in the API gateway which will help you direct the traffic based on your environment. We will use an API gateway to host Lambda endpoints.

Lambda (15)

AWS Lambda is a fully managed service that revolutionized the way you can host your application in the cloud. It is also termed serverless computing because you don't need to provide any server to host your application. However, in the backend, AWS does host your application on the server inside the containers (it abstracts the implementation details from the developers). Lambda needs zero administration and scales automatically. The developers can now focus only on their code and the rest is taken care of by Lambda. The user pays for the Lambda configuration (CPU and memory) and for the time it runs. Initially, when Lambda got introduced, the developers used it for simple isolated functions like polling messages from the queue and passed them to another service. But as Lambda got mature, developers began using it to host the backend services with the help of API gateway.

However, there are a few limitations as follows:

- **Cold Start**: When the function responds to an event, there is a delay for the function to execute. The delay can be up to 10 sec based on your package size. To overcome this issue, most of the developers tried to keep Lambda warm by calling it after a specific time. Suppose if you configured Lambda running time to 15 minutes, then configure a CloudWatch event to trigger that lambda every 10 mins. This way, Lambda is always available and can be used in critical applications.

- **Limits**: Lambda processing payload size limit is 6 MB. The API gateway payload size limit is 10 MB. The maximum configured timeout in Lambda is 15 minutes. After 15 minutes, the existing Lambda instance will terminate and a new instance will start (this is where the cold start occurs).

Relational Database Service (16)

According to AWS, Amazon Relational Database Service (Amazon RDS) is a web service that makes it easier to set up, operate, and scale a relational database in the AWS Cloud. Currently, AWS RDS supports MySQL, MariaDB, PostgreSQL, Oracle, and Microsoft SQL servers. The basic building block of RDS is DB Instances. When you provision a database in RDS, you need to configure DB instances and define the compute configuration as needed. The compute configuration (CPU and memory capacity) is determined by the DB instance class. The pricing varies based on the instance class. You can run a DB Instance to either public or private subnet. AWS RDS manages backup, patching, and recovery which makes it highly available. Usually, we put RDS instances inside a private subnet so that it cannot access the data from the outside world. In this book, we are going to provision MySQL RDS instance inside a private subnet, and to access it, we will use bastion host.

> Note: A bastion host is a server whose purpose is to provide access to a private network from an external network, such as the Internet.

Simple Storage Service (17)

Amazon **Simple Storage Service (S3)** is cloud storage maintained and accessed over the internet. Using S3, you can store and retrieve a vast amount of data, either programmatically or through an AWS console. S3 has two primary entities, buckets, and objects. It stores objects inside a bucket. You create a bucket and whatever you store inside that bucket is an object. S3 is a global service, and each bucket must have a unique name that doesn't exist in any other AWS account in any region.

Elastic Cache (18)

An elastic cache is a fully managed service that allows you to set up open-source, compatible, in-memory data stores in the cloud. Currently, it is offering Redis and Memcached. In this book, we will use the Redis cache to store rarely changeable data and connection strings. Redis stands for Remote Dictionary Server and is an open-source, fast, in-memory data store software. Since all the Redis data resides in the memory, it significantly reduces the data access latency to microseconds as compared to the database. AWS Redis cache is simple to use, highly available, scalable, and can replicate to multiple servers. To clear Redis cache data, you need to restart the instance.

Monitoring (19)

We will talk about two monitoring services in this section, are **CloudWatch** and **X-Ray.** We will use these in this book. AWS CloudWatch is a central log service that monitors AWS resources and applications in real-time. You can create alarms that watch metrics and send notifications automatically in case of a threshold breach. It stores CloudWatch data as log streams inside the log groups. The X-Ray helps developers to analyze and debug distributed applications using a microservice architecture. With the help of an X-Ray, you can trace your application data flow. Using a service map, create a group using a filter based on the environment. Use HTTP status code to filter out records. In the following chapter, we will see how to add an X-Ray to your ASP.NET Core Web API project.

Some important services

The following services are important for almost any application you will host on AWS.

Identity and Access Management

Identity and Access Management (IAM) manages individual and group users to access AWS resources and defines the level of access. Each user in AWS must have IAM policies to grant permission. There are different parts of IAM:

- **User**: IAM user is an identity with associated credentials and policies. It associates each IAM user with each AWS account. When you create a new account in AWS, you will be the root user. Root users are like superusers who have all the access. From IAM, you can create other users and groups and start assigning permissions. When you create users, by default, it doesn't have any permission. You must assign users either to a group or assign permission explicitly.

- **Groups**: Groups are the collections of users that have similar permissions or policies associated with them.

- **Policies**: Policies are JSON documents that define the services a user can access and their level of access. Policies are of three types:

  o **Managed**: Managed policies are created and managed by AWS.

  o **Custom**: You can create and manage your policies. You can assign custom policies to users, groups, and roles within your account.

  o **Inline**: Inline policies are embedded into the IAM of a single user, group, or role to which it applies. If you delete that user, role, or group, the inline policy attached to it will also get deleted.

- **Roles**: Roles are assigned to AWS resources. The role allows the AWS resources to access other resources on your behalf. An EC2 instance cannot access the S3 bucket by default unless you assign an S3 role to that EC2 instance. Using roles, the user doesn't have to configure his AWS credentials in every EC2 instance to access other AWS resources.

Note: Always use Multi-Factor Authentication (MFA) to secure your AWS account. AWS recommends using managed policies over inline policies.

Parameter Store

According to AWS, the AWS systems manager parameter store provides secure, hierarchical storage for configuration, data management, and secrets management. You can store data, such as passwords, database strings, **Amazon Machine Image (AMI)** IDs, and license codes as the parameter values. You can store values as plain text or encrypted data. However, there is a maximum limit of 1000 requests/sec. You can change the default limit to the max limit from the `Parameter Setting` tab.

Tags

AWS tags allow users to add custom labels to their AWS resources which makes it easier to manage and search resources based on the environment, owner, or any other criteria. If multiple teams work in your organization, then tagging AWS resources based on team id helps to identify the resources that are being used. Also, when you have multiple environments, like DEV, TEST, PROD, tagging based on the environment allows filtering the resources in the billing dashboard and the cost associated with it. It is always a good practice to tag your resources for audit purposes.

SQS

SQS stands for Simple Queuing Service. It is a fully managed queuing service that enables decoupling, scales microservices, and distributes applications. AWS introduced SQS in 2004. It was the first service available in AWS. Using SQS, you can design fault-tolerant and independent microservice applications. It can act as a middleware between the microservices communication so that if any of the microservices is down, the message will not get lost but stored in a queue. There are two types of queues:

- **Standard Queues**: It guarantees that message is delivered at least once but is out of order. However, duplicate messages can be delivered out of order.

- **First In First Out (FIFO)**: It delivers a message in order and follows the *"exactly once"* processing feature.

SNS

Simple Notification Service (SNS) is a fully managed, auto-scale messaging service for decoupling communication. It enables the creation of modern and decoupled systems using the publish/subscribe pattern. SNS can fan out a communication to queues, Lambda, and EC2 instances for parallel processing. It also helps monitor the applications by subscribing to the live data. SNS can also deliver notifications by SMS or email.

Step Functions

Step functions are used to orchestrate complex business logic flows using Lambda. If your application contains multiple Lambdas, each executing a single task and you want to orchestrate them to accomplish a task, then step function is the right option. Step function provides functionality like retry, error handling, monitoring, workflow, and ensures that each step is executed in the correct order. Step functions can be scheduled as a background job using CloudWatch.

Conclusion

In this chapter, we discussed AWS terminologies and some of its services which we will use in the upcoming chapters. After going through the chapter, you got a fair amount of understanding of why companies are moving towards the cloud. The main reasons are cost-effectiveness and flexibility. You follow the pay-as-you-go pricing model. You can use any service anytime without worrying about the servers.

You can add or remove the servers as needed. AWS changed the way we develop and host applications. Most of the modern applications are being developed keeping cloud computing into consideration so that the applications can scale easily. In the next chapter, we will look at the Microservice design patterns used while designing an application.

Points to Remember

- Each geographical location in AWS is termed a **region**. Each region has multiple **availability zones**.

- Subnets can be private or public. Attach internet gateway to the subnet to make it public. NAT gateway is always attached to the private subnet.

- EC2 instances are one of the basic building blocks of AWS. You have full control over the EC2 instances you provision.

- Security groups are applied to the resources inside the subnet and NACL's are attached to the subnets.

- Use load balancer and Auto Scaling combination to make applications highly available, scalable, and fault tolerant.

- Route 53 is a highly scalable and available Domain Name System (DNS) web service.

- API gateway is a managed service where you configure both the stateful (WebSocket) and the stateless (REST and HTTP) services.

- AWS Lambda is a fully managed and serverless compute service.

- S3 is a global service and bucket names should be unique irrespective of region in an AWS account.

- CloudWatch is the central AWS logging platform that monitors all the services and X-Ray is used to monitor distributed applications, like microservices.

- IAM is used to grant service access to users.

Multiple choice questions

1. **Subnets are a part of:**
   a) Region
   b) Availably zone
   c) VPC

2. **VPC spreads across multiple:**
   a) Region
   b) Availably zone
   c) Areas

3. **IAM stands for:**
   a) Identity and Access Management
   b) Information and Access Management
   c) Identity and Approve Management

4. **What is the pricing model available for EC2 instances?**
   a) On-Demand
   b) Reserve
   c) Spot
   d) All the above

5. **What are the two primary entities of S3?**
   a) Bucket
   b) Objects
   c) A and B
   d) Only A

6. **AWS tags allow users to add custom labels to their AWS resources.**
   a) True
   b) False

Answer

1. b
2. b
3. a
4. c
5. c
6. a

Chapter 4

Microservices Patterns

One man's crappy software is another man's full-time job.

- - Jessica Gaston

Introduction

The preceding quote by Jessica Gaston is very much true in the software world. I too come across a software that was written by developers (who didn't work for the company anymore) and a team was later assigned to maintain that software who found it hard to change or add new functionalities. Maybe the developers write shoddy code (which is working) either because they didn't have enough experience or because of time constraints. In both the scenarios, companies spend considerable amount of money and time to maintain these softwares. To avoid developers writing unmaintainable, hard-to-understand code, we should refer to the design patterns and follow the industry-approved coding standards (coding standards often differ based on the language used). Design patterns are solutions to a commonly occurring problem. It accelerates the software release cycle and helps to maintain code in the future. In this chapter, we will summarize some important design patterns used in microservices. As we have already discussed in the previous chapters, microservices are independent of each other and can be deployed separately. So, these patterns help us to find the solution for some of the common problems like microservice communication, deployment strategy, decomposition, and resilience to failure.

Structure

Patterns:

- Aggregator pattern
- API gateway
- Distributed and shared database
- Command and query responsibility segregation
- Saga pattern
    - o Two-phase commits
- Strangler pattern
- Circuit breaker pattern
- Service discovery
- Blue-green deployment
- Bulkhead pattern
- Chain responsibility pattern
- Branch pattern

Objective

In this chapter, you will get to know about microservice patterns, the problems it solves, and how it can increase your application performance.

At the end of this chapter, you will have a better of understanding of microservice patterns and when to apply these.

Patterns

A software design pattern solves a commonly occurring problem in the software design. To overcome these common challenges in any development project, developers usually refer to the design patterns. The following patterns are few microservice patterns that we can leverage while design microservices.

Aggregator pattern

Suppose you have 100 microservices and your web application wants to show a consolidated report to users by collecting the data from different microservices. So, your client application queries microservices and consolidates the data at its end to show it to the end-users. This approach will have potential performance issues, as the client must query each microservice to get the relevant data and aggregate it at its end.

In this type of scenario, the aggregator pattern comes to the rescue. You can create an aggregator microservice that will collect the relevant data from the concerned microservice and store it in its database. Any change in the microservice data on which the aggregator relied upon will raise an event to an aggregator and the aggregator will update its data store. This pattern is beneficial when you need output by combining data from different microservices. You can expose the aggregators as a REST endpoint and the client can call it to get the composed data.

The following diagram represents microservice A and microservice B publishing changes to the message bus and the aggregator microservice subscribing to those changes to update its database:

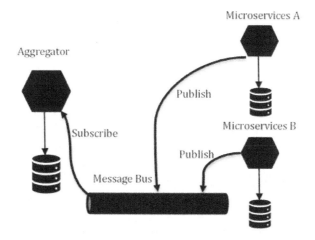

Figure 4.1: Aggregator pattern

API Gateway

There are different ways a client can call microservices. One approach is to call the microservice directly. This approach is straight forward and is efficient for a small set of microservices. With complex applications, this approach has a significant issue like chatty interface, non-centralized authorization, data transformation, and no data payload optimization based on the client type. With microservice endpoint changes, we must deploy the client application as well. This introduces tight coupling between the client and the server.

The following diagram depicts the interaction with microservices without API gateway.

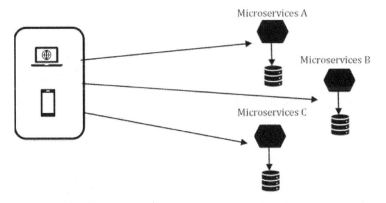

Figure 4.2: Microservice communication without Gateway

For these scenarios, we can use API gateway which acts as a façade for a distributed system, and as a reverse proxy that hides the complexity of microservice routing. In the case of microservice service endpoint changes, we only need to change the mapping on API gateway without client deployment. Now, microservices behind API gateway can be scaled in or out at will. The API gateway also provides additional functionalities like logging, centralized authentication/authorization, secure communication, service discovery, response caching, rate limiting, data compression, data transformation, and so on. We can also create a separate API gateway based on the client type to configure data compression and transformation as needed.

The following diagram shows different clients communicating with microservices using their respective API gateways, making it resilient to failure and customizable.

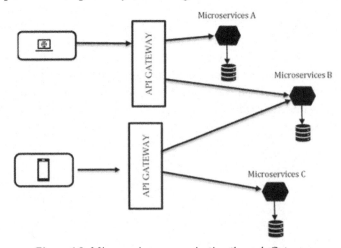

Figure 4.3: Microservice communication through Gateway

Distributed and shared database

Monolithic applications use a shared database where all the services communicate to a single database server. It tightly couples services to each other and the changes in the database model can affect multiple services. A shared database is considered as an antipattern for microservice that defeats an autonomous deployment characteristic of microservices. But, at the beginning of the monolithic to microservice transition, when we don't have enough business knowledge to segregate the database model, the developers often start with a shared database. Start designing your microservice using a shared database and try to map it to tables in a way such that it will have minimum side effect while segregating the database according to microservices in the future.

The following diagram shows the interaction of microservices with a single database, and the next diagram shows the interaction of microservices with the distributed database.

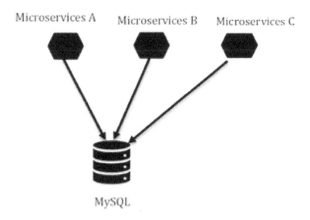

Figure 4.4: *Shared Database*

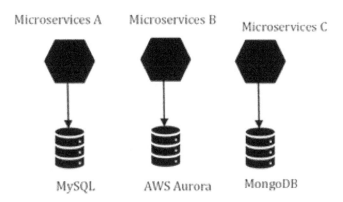

Figure 4.5: *Distributed Database*

Ideally, each microservice should have its database for autonomous deployment and loosely coupled architecture. The primary advantage of a distributed database is that a change in the table structure of one microservice doesn't affect the other microservice. You can scale the databases independently, use different database types, like SQL, NO-SQL, as per need, and use different database vendors, like SQL server, MySQL, AWS Aurora. However, the maintenance and monitoring of distributed databases require additional effort. Also, patterns like aggregators come in handy in these types of designs.

Command and Query Responsibility Segregation

Usually, when we design a system, we create a database model and use it for both read and write operations. However, if you consider at the time of write, we deal with the entity but at the time of read, we need the aggregated data. **Command and Query Responsibility Segregation** (CQRS) is a pattern that separates the model for reading and writing data. It divides the system into two separate categories:

Queries: Return results from a system

Command: Mutate the system

In simple terms, CQRS separates the read operation from the write one. The model in a read operation can differ from the write. For example, **GetOrderById**, **GetOrderDetails** come under query and **CreateOrder**, **UpdateOrder** come under command.

The following diagram shows the microservice having separate databases for reading and writing:

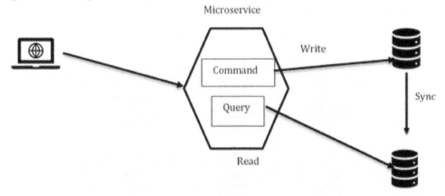

Figure 4.6: CQRS communication

One of the challenges of CQRS is data synchronization. When we add/update records in the write database, data synchronization is needed to the read database.

This can be done in multiple ways. However, in our case of MySQL RDS, we can create a read replica database. It will replicate any changes in the master database to the read replica database. Sometimes, the developers further segregate the CQRS microservice into two microservice, one for write and one for read. Using this approach, you can create separate data contexts and design models for each microservice as often read operations are more encountered than the write ones. Also, the microservices can be scaled independently. However, the maintenance of these systems with so many microservices can sometimes become a nightmare. So, decide diligently before you think of applying CQRS in your microservice design.

Saga pattern

In a monolithic application, the ACID properties are retained because of a single database architecture. However, in microservices, atomicity (all instructions in a transaction either run successfully or rollback in case of any failure), consistency (integrity constrain of data should be maintained pre/post-transaction), and isolation (intermediate transaction state should be invisible) are difficult to maintain because of the distributed databases. Two patterns are used to resolve this issue:

- 2PC (two-phase commit)
- Saga

Two-phase commit

2PC has two phases, **prepare** and **commit**. In the preparation phase, the coordinator asks all the microservice to prepare. Once all are prepared, the coordinator asks them to commit.

The following diagram shows successful 2PC transactions:

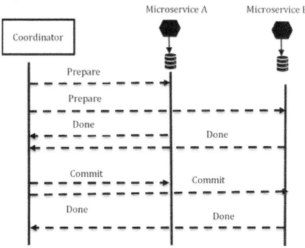

Figure 4.7: *2pc transactions*

The main drawback of this pattern is that this is synchronous. During the process, if a single microservice fails, the coordinator will initiate the rollback process and the whole transaction will get rolled back. If there are *n* microservice and the last one failed, then *n-1* microservice will get rolled back. This will significantly reduce the performance of the application. Also, this violates the data isolation. The customer will see the data changes related to microservice and then suddenly, the data gets deleted because of the roll back.

The following diagram shows failed 2PC transactions:

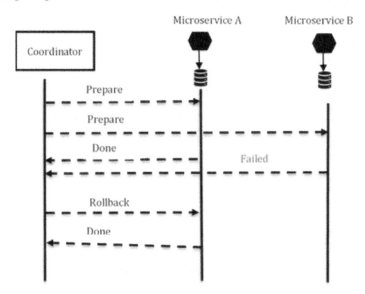

Figure 4.8: 2pc rollback transactions

Saga pattern

This pattern tries to solve the 2PC problems. Saga patterns are asynchronous and the application doesn't wait for the transaction to complete. There are two ways to implement the saga pattern:

- **Choreography**: Each microservice transaction publish domain events that trigger other microservice transactions. They can share events over the REST endpoints, or queues, or message bus. The disadvantage of this approach is that it becomes complex in a large application and becomes hard to maintain.

The following diagram shows the saga choreography interactions:

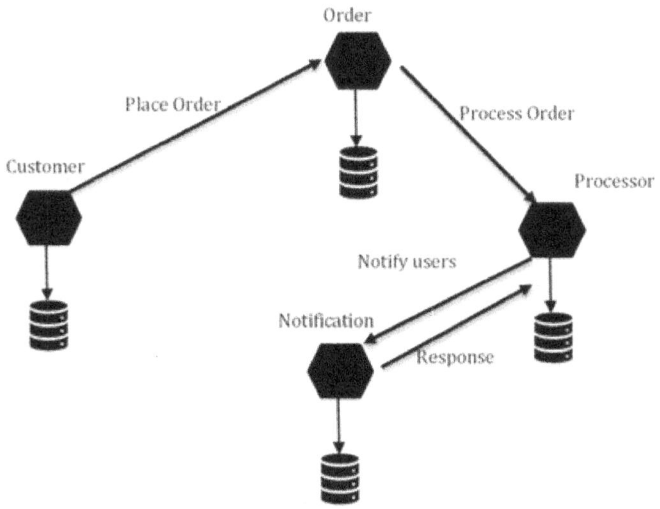

Order
Place Order
Process Order
Customer
Processor
Notify users
Notification
Response

Figure 4.9: *Saga Choreography communication*

- **Orchestration**: The orchestrator controls the transactions among different microservices. The advantage of this approach is that the data isolation and coordination among microservices increase the performance.

  In AWS, the step function service can be used to implement the saga orchestrator, which controls the data consistency among microservices.

  The following diagram shows the saga orchestration interactions:

Customer
Message Broker
Validate Order
Orchestrator
Customer
Processor
Process Order
Notify users
Notification

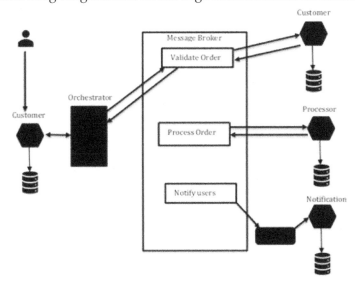

Figure 4.10: *Saga Orchestra communication*

Strangler pattern

Replacing monolithic applications with microservices is a huge task, and often leads to unmaintainable issues. To handle this scenario, a strangler pattern is used where we segregate the monolithic application into microservice based on different domains. In this pattern, two applications run side-by-side and incrementally migrate the functionality of monolithic service with the application and microservices that eventually shuts down the monolithic application.

Circuit breaker

In a microservice application, one microservice often calls another microservice synchronously. Because of various reasons like network latency, exception, timeout, etc. the response fails. The calling microservice will either retry after a timeout or pass the exception to the upper layers. Eventually, this might cause an issue when the load increases. Each call to a failing microservice will hold up significant resources like memory, threads, database connection, and can lead to cascading failure. A circuit breaker pattern is used to resolve these issues. This pattern will increase the microservice resiliency and fault tolerance. The circuit breaker acts as a proxy for the synchronous microservice communication. A circuit breaker has three states:

- **Closed**: When everything is normal, the circuit breaker is in the closed state.

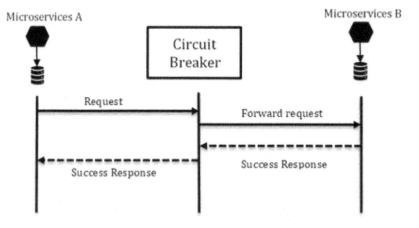

Figure 4.11: Closed State

- **Open**: When in the open state, the circuit breaker responds with an error message on behalf of the fault service.

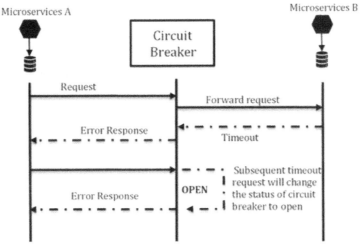

Figure 4.12: *Open State*

- **Half-Open**: After a period, the circuit breaker will check the whether the service is up or not. If down, it will change the state to open, otherwise to closed.

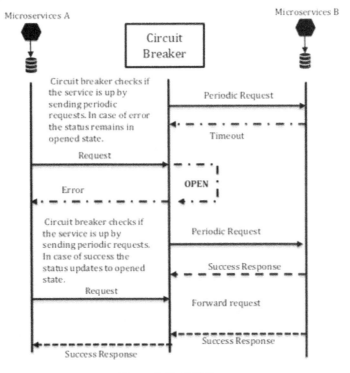

Figure 4.13: *Half-Open*

Service discovery pattern

As we know we build modern applications on microservices for advantages like loosening, resiliency, language agnostics, and independent deployment. However, one of the main challenges of microservice architectures is to discover the service and interact with each other. The simple solution is to bypass the service discovery and hardcode the service endpoint with which we want to communicate in our code. However, the problem with this approach is if somehow the endpoint changes or shuts down, the communication fails. The service discovery responsibility is to map the service endpoints and use them for both inter and intra communications. Service discovery is of two types:

Client-side service discovery

Here, the client is responsible to discover the endpoint it wants to communicate. For the sake of analogy, let us suppose you have some problem with your phone and you want to call the customer care. To get the customer care number or email id, you search the Google. Here, you as a client, try to get the information from Google (service discovery) and initiate the connection. The disadvantage of this solution is the client must first discover and then call the service. This extra hop can add latency to the call.

Server-side service discovery

Here, the client sends the request to the server and the it is the server's responsibility to discover the subsequent endpoints. Let us understand this with an analogy. Suppose you want to talk to the CEO of a big organization. You call the CEO's secretary and the secretary forwards your call to the CEO. Here, the secretary acts as a server-side discovery who knows the CEO's extension line, phone number, and whether he is available or not. You don't know any of this. All you have to do is call the secretary. Similarly, in AWS, when we provision our EC2 instances behind a load balancer, the load balancer checks the health of the instances and forwards the request to a healthy instance. If any instance gets unhealthy, it will get replaced by the Auto Scaling group and the traffic will go uninterrupted. The API gateway also acts as a server-side service discovery hosting AWS Lambda instances. The client doesn't care about the Lambda instance endpoint. All it must do is call the endpoint to expose by API gateway and get the response. The API gateway does the heavy lifting of managing the Lambda instance mapping and availability.

Blue-green deployment pattern

In the blue-green deployment, you need to maintain two identical copies of the application's production infrastructure, one designated as blue and the other designated as green. At any point in time, only one environment is live, say blue. When you plan a new release deployed in a green environment, test it, route the traffic to green, and make it live. After going live, if something fails, you can quickly switch to blue. One of the advantages of the blue-green deployment is you can quickly switch between the environments, making it resilient to failure. However, this can add extra cost and maintenance to your organization. Now, you must maintain two separate identical environments having one environment idle.

In AWS, the developers use cloud formation to create an infrastructure template. The formation template is Infrastructure as Code (IaC) that contains all the resources with configurations needed for your application. Using the cloud formation, you can maintain a different version of your organization's infrastructure in source control and use it to quickly spawn up your application production infrastructure in AWS. Cloud formation templates can be used efficiently in case of blue-green deployment. You can delete your idle environment (which reduces cost) once the release is done. For subsequent release, run the cloud formation template to provision a new environment and follow blue-green deployment. It is good to create environments in separate VPCs because deleting VPC will remove all the services provisioned underlying it.

The following diagram shows the swapping of stable and tested server interacting with customers after every release:

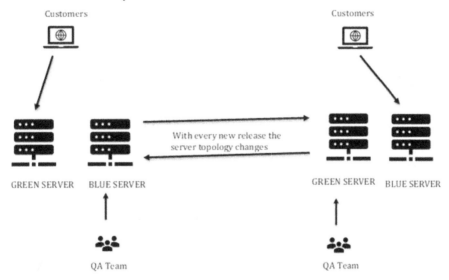

Figure 4.14: Blue-Green Deployment

Bulkhead pattern

The bulkhead pattern is used to isolate failure in one part of the system and prevent it to propagate to the entire system which may eventually take the whole system down. In microservice design, developers often overlook this pattern, but later, it can become a major issue with respect to the performance of the application. To overcome this issue, there are options available like throttling (provide a fixed number of connections to a microservice). Also, you can define timeout (using circuit breaker) or rate limit (number of requests in a time interval). Another option is to introduce a queue between microservice communication which will limit the output flow, and in case of failure, will store the messages for reprocessing.

Chained responsibility pattern

In this pattern, the microservice communication occurs in a chained fashion, calling one after the other, and finally generating the desired output. Since communication happens synchronously, it is recommended to use a small chain. This pattern is useful when the microservices calls are not mutually exclusive and require structuring data in a specific format.

The following diagram shows the chained microservices interacting synchronously with each other.

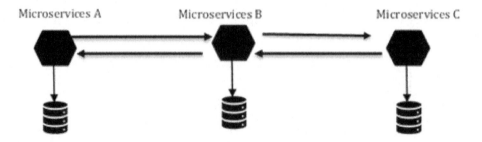

Figure 4.15: *Chained Pattern*

Branch pattern

In this design pattern, one microservice can simultaneously call more than one microservices and process data. Unlike chain patterns, it is not synchronous, but passes the request to independent microservices. This pattern is useful when you want to fetch data from two mutually exclusive microservice simultaneously.

The following diagram shows branched microservices interacting asynchronously with each other.

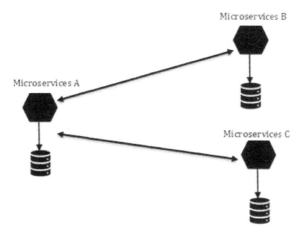

Figure 4.16: *Branch Pattern*

Conclusion

While partitioning monolithic to Microservices you have a tradeoff between consistency and availability known as CAP theorem. Based on the business functionality, requirements, and context either of the two will dominate the other. Microservice is not a solution to all problems and considers it only when it is required. Before deciding on a Microservice ask yourself questions like what the problems are Microservice will solve, what will be the result. Do not implement Microservice blindly for the sake of learning new technology. If not properly designed Microservice can become a nightmare for your team. In this chapter, I discussed a few practices to follow to help you go through some of the limitations which you need to consider while hosting Microservice to lambda. In the following chapter, we will go through a Microservice and try to implement the concepts we have learned until now.

Points to remember

- A software design pattern is a solution to a commonly occurring problem in the context of software design.

- The API gateway acts as a façade for a distributed system and as a reverse proxy which hides the complexity of routing.

- A shared database can be used at the initial level to segregate monolithic applications to microservice.

- The distributed database helps to achieve autonomous deployment and loosely coupled architecture.

- CQRS divides the system into two separate categories, queries (return results from a system) and command (mutate the system).

- Saga patterns are asynchronous and the application doesn't wait for the transaction to complete. These are of two types, orchestrator and choreography.

- Circuit breaker pattern will increase the microservice resiliency and fault tolerance.

- Service discovery is of two types, client-side and server-side.

- Blue-green deployment maintains two identical copies of the application's production infrastructure, one designated as blue and the other designated as green, to make it resilient to failure.

- Bulkhead pattern is used to isolate failure in one part of the system and prevent it to propagate to the entire system which may eventually take the whole system down.

- In the chained responsibility pattern, microservice communication occurs in a chained fashion calling one after the other synchronously.

- In a branch pattern, one microservice can simultaneously call more than one microservices and process the data asynchronously.

- The API gateway response limit timeout is 30 seconds.

- Lambda payload handling limit is 6 MB.

- Lambda incurs delay every time a new Lambda instance spawns up. This delay is known as **Lambda cold start**.

- Use Lambda layers and try to host outside VPC (if possible) to reduce Lambda cold start.

- HTTP2 is a major revision of Http1.0 and is used to improve the performance, speed, and efficiency of the web.

- **Open Data Protocol (OData)** is an application-level protocol to interact with data via the REST interface.

- AWS step function is a serverless function orchestrator that orchestrates multiple serverless functions to achieve business functionalities.

- CloudWatch is the centralized logging platform for AWS where AWS services log their information.

Multiple choice questions

1. **Which pattern is used to break monolithic to microservices?**

    a. Circuit breaker

    b. Bulkhead

    c. Strangler

2. **Chained responsibility pattern is**

    a. Synchronous

    b. Asynchronous

    c. None

3. **Which pattern is used to block issues propagating to the entire system?**

    a. Circuit Breaker

    b. Bulkhead

    c. Strangler

4. **What is the API gateway response limit?**

    a. 60

    b. 40

    c. 35

    d. 30

5. **What are the features of HTTP2?**

    a. Compression of headers

    b. A binary protocol

    c. None of the above

6. **What is the limit of Lambda payload for processing?**

    a. 8 MB

    b. 10 MB

    c. 6 MB

    d. None of the above

Answer

1. c
2. a
3. b
4. d
5. a, b
6. c

CHAPTER 5
Serverless Paradigm

No server is easier to manage than no server.

-Werner Vogels (Amazon CTO)

Introduction

Nowadays, companies are eager to move to the cloud, not just because of pricing, but also to overcome infrastructure maintenance. Cloud computing moves a lot of responsibilities from developers (especially operational) to itself so that the developers are more focused and agile to their core products and need not worry about the infrastructure. Serverless computing is one such initiative and has gained massive popularity when AWS first introduced it. It is the architecture of the cloud which moves operational responsibility from developers to the cloud and provides high availability/scalability. In serverless computing, the developers need not worry about server provisioning, operating system, and capacity. Different cloud providers have different names for serverless computing. For example, in Microsoft Azure, it is called Azure function, in Google, Cloud function, and in AWS, it is called the Lambda function. In this chapter, we will go through the practical implementation of our first microservice and see how to deploy in AWS Lambda. We will also try to recall some of the concepts from the previous chapters and apply them here.

Structure

- Configuring AWS
- Overview of a sample Serverless application
    - o Infrastructure project
    - o Domain project
    - o API project
    - o Configuring startup
    - o Serverless template
- Get custom domain
- Create a self-signed certificate
- Add a certificate to AWS Certificate Manager
- Configure API gateway
- Deploy Lambda function
- Configure Route 53
- Final step

Objective

In this chapter, you will gather enough practical knowledge on microservice implementation and deployment. If you are new to AWS, it is highly recommended to refer to AWS documentation along with this chapter for any doubts.

By the end of this chapter, you will be able to create, deploy, and run microservice securely on AWS Lambda. You will also be able to implement OpenAPI specifications on your microservice project.

Configuring AWS

In this section, we will discuss how to install AWS CLI in your local development machine.

1. Install AWS CLI for Windows by visiting the official AWS website: **https://docs.aws.amazon.com/cli/latest/userguide/install-cliv2-windows.html**. After installing, open the command prompt and use the aws --version to check if everything is installed properly, as shown in the following screenshot:

Figure 5.1: AWS Version

2. Now, create an account in the AWS Management Console and go to the IAM (Identity and Access Management) service. Under IAM, create the Lambda_ execute_role which we will use for lambda deployment, and attach the following policies :

- AWSLambdaFullAccess
- AmazonS3FullAccess

3. After you have successfully created your account, configure AWS on your machine by typing aws configure on your terminal.

Provide the details of your AWS account, like the access key, secret access key while you configure AWS on your machine, as shown in the following screenshot:

Figure 5.2: AWS Configure

Note: When you create a new account, it will be the root account. Make sure to create an IAM user and assign an MFA device to each account. Also, create an access key to configure AWS on your local machine. It is recommended by AWS to not use your root account for your day-to-day work.

Overview of a sample serverless application

Now, we will create our first serverless application microservice **CountryCapital**. This microservice exposes an endpoint that will accept the country and return the capital of that country. Before you get started, you must be informed that we are not going to use a database with this microservice to store or retrieve country information to avoid unnecessary code complications. However, a repository pattern has been introduced where the application doesn't know how the data is being handled by the repository layer. It only knows how to delegate responsibility to the repository layer and abstraction has been added around data processing so that in the future you can change the way it processes data without changing other areas of application. Don't get disheartened by the simple content. This microservice makes you familiar with some basic configurations needed when you develop microservices using Lambda. You will also learn some important concepts which will be useful in the subsequent chapters. We will structure our solution following some DDD rules. To achieve this, we will create four main projects:

- **Microservices.CountryCapital.API** (**Application Layer**): This project will have ASP.NET Core Web API endpoints which is an entry point for your application. This contains API contracts/implementation.

- **Microservices.CountryCapital.Domain** (**Domain Layer**): This project will have a domain entity model, POCO value and entity objects, domain entity classes with data, and behavior. This is where you will define your business logic and is the heart of the application. Ideally, the domain should be independent and doesn't reference any project.

- **Microservices.CountryCapital.Infrastructure** (**Infrastructure layer**): This is the infrastructure layer of the project which will have the data persistence logic using ORMs and other infrastructure-related implementation, like SQS, logging, and so on.

- **Microservices.CountryCapital.Services**: This project is used as a mediator between the controller and other projects. The controller will pass the request message to the service layer and the service layer's responsibility is to get the relevant data and map the properties to the API response model.

The following diagram shows the reference map, where the arrow points out from the project means the destination project has a reference in the originating project. For example, **Microservices.CountryCapital.API** has three outgoing arrows referencing **Microservices.CountryCapital.Domain, Microservices. CountryCapital.Services** and **Microservices.CountryCapital. Infrastructure**. However, if you look closely, **Microservices.CountryCapital. Domain** doesn't have any outgoing arrow. This means this project is independent and doesn't have any references from other projects. This is helpful because in the future when you want to migrate to a different .NET Core application, you can just lift and shift the domain project to that application. If you plan to write in a different language other than C#, you need to translate the domain to that language. Another advantage is the unit test. Your domain project should have a code coverage of nearly 80%-90%:

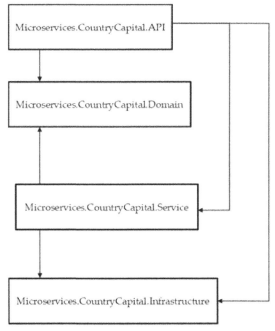

Figure 5.3: *Dependency Map*

Let's start by creating a blank solution. After the solution is created, we will create an API project. Right-click on it and select **New Project**. Under New Project, select AWS serverless application (.NET Core – C#) project. Now, we will create a domain, infrastructure, and service C# library projects.

> Refer to *chapter 2, Introduction to ASP.NET Core Web API,* where we discussed creating C# Lambda projects in detail. In this chapter, we will discuss additional components of the lambda application needed to build microservices using .NET Core 3.1.

Infrastructure project

Here, we will add logic related to infrastructure like database, AWS Simple Storage Service (S3), queues, topics, and so on. In this example, in our infrastructure project, we have two repositories, file, and S3.

Add **IRepository** to serve two purposes, first for the dependency injection, and second, if in the future we need another storage mechanism, we can use this interface to implement the methods obeying the open-closed principle.

```
1.    using Microservices.CountryCapital.Infrastructure.Models;
2.    using System.Linq;
3.    using System.Threading.Tasks;
```

```
4.
5.    namespace Microservices.CountryCapital.Infrastructure
6.    {
7.        public interface IRepository
8.        {
9.            Task<IQueryable<Country>> GetCountriesAsync();
10.           Task<Country> FindCountryByIdAsync(int countryId);
11.       }
12.   }
```

The following country model is used to map data in the repository. There are also added behaviours to the model, like **isValid()** to validate the data retrieved from the data source. By adding behaviours to the model, you can convert an anemic model into a rich model. An anemic model is an entity that lacks business logic and only contains a collection of getters and setters.

```
1.    using System;
2.    using System.Collections.Generic;
3.    using System.Text;
4.
5.    namespace Microservices.CountryCapital.Infrastructure.Models
6.    {
7.        public class Country
8.        {
9.            public int Id {get; set;}
10.           public string Name {get; set;}
11.           public string Code {get; set;}
12.           public string Capital {get; set;}
13.
14.           public Boolean isValid()
15.           {
16.               return Id != 0;
17.           }
18.
19.
20.       }
21.   }
```

IRepository implementation for file storage. In this class, we will read data stored in a file.

```
1.    using System;
2.    using System.Collections.Generic;
3.    using System.IO;
4.    using System.Linq;
5.    using System.Threading.Tasks;
6.    using Microservices.CountryCapital.Infrastructure.Models;
7.
8.    namespace Microservices.CountryCapital.Infrastructure
9.        public class FileRepository: IRepository
10.       {
11.           public async Task<Country> FindCountryByIdAsync(int
      countryId)
12.           {
13.               var content = GetFileData();
14.               return content.FirstOrDefault(x => x.Id ==
      countryId);
15.           }
16.
17.           public async Task<IQueryable<Country>>
      GetCountriesAsync()
18.           {
19.               var content = GetFileData();
20.               return content.AsQueryable();
        }
21.           private static List<Country> GetFileData()
22.           {
23.               string content = String.Empty;
24.               var dir = AppContext.BaseDirectory;
25.               using (var sr = new StreamReader(Path.Combine(dir,
      "TestFile.txt")))
26.               {
27.                   content = sr.ReadToEnd();
28.               }
```

```
29.
30.                  return Newtonsoft.Json.JsonConvert.
       DeserializeObject<List<Country>>(content);
31.
32.           }
33.        }
34.     }
```

IRepository implementation for S3. In this class, we will read data from a file stored in an AWS S3 storage location.

```
1.     using System;
2.     using System.Collections.Generic;
3.     using System.IO;
4.     using System.Linq;
5.     using System.Threading.Tasks;
6.     using Amazon;
7.     using Amazon.S3;
8.     using Amazon.S3.Model;
9.     using Microservices.CountryCapital.Infrastructure.Models;
10.
11.    namespace Microservices.CountryCapital.Infrastructure
12.        public class S3Repository: IRepository
13.        {
14.            private static IAmazonS3 client = new
       AmazonS3Client(RegionEndpoint.USEast1);
15.
16.            public async Task<Country> FindCountryByIdAsync(int
       countryId)
17.            {
18.                var content = await GetFileDataAsync();
19.                return content.FirstOrDefault(x => x.Id ==
       countryId);
20.            }
21.
22.            public async Task<IQueryable<Country>>
       GetCountriesAsync()
```

```
23.              {
24.                  var content = await GetFileDataAsync();
25.                  return content.AsQueryable();
26.              }
27.
28.          private static async Task<List<Country>>
      GetFileDataAsync()
29.              {
30.                  string responseBody = "";
31.                  try
32.                  {
33.                      GetObjectRequest request = new GetObjectRequest
34.                      {
35.                          BucketName = "countrycapital",
36.                          Key = "TestFile.txt"
37.                      };
38.                      using (GetObjectResponse response = await client.
      GetObjectAsync(request))
39.                      using (Stream responseStream = response.
      ResponseStream)
40.                      using (StreamReader reader = new
      StreamReader(responseStream))
41.                      {
42.
43.                          responseBody = reader.ReadToEnd(); // Now you
      process the response body.
44.                      }
45.                  }
46.                  catch (AmazonS3Exception e)
47.                  {
48.                      // If bucket or object does not exist
49.                      Console.WriteLine("Error encountered ***.
      Message:'{0}' when reading object", e.Message);
50.                  }
51.                  catch (Exception e)
```

```
52.                    {
53.                        Console.WriteLine("Unknown encountered on server.
       Message:'{0}' when reading object", e.Message);
54.                    }
55.                    return Newtonsoft.Json.JsonConvert.
       DeserializeObject<List<Country>>(responseBody);
56.
57.            }
58.        }
59.    }
```

If you check the preceding code, you will notice the following:

- We have implemented the IRepository interface in both classes.

   We have retrieved the data from different sources in different scenarios.

Content of **TestFile.txt** used as a data source

```
[{"Id":1,"Name":"UnitedStates","Code":"US","Capital":"Washington"},
{"Id":2,"Name":"India","Code":"IN","Capital":"NewDelhi"},
{"Id":3, "Name":"Russia", "Code":"RUS","Capital":"Moscow"},
{"Id":4,"Name":"Japan","Code":"JP", "Capital":"Tokyo"},{"Id":5,"Name":
"Mexico","Code":"MX","Capital": "MexicoCity"}]
```

Domain project

This is the heart of your application that contains business logic and business validation. You must spend most of your valuable time here. Also, as discussed, this project shouldn't have any reference to any other project of the solution. Your domain project should be independent and should sustain independently. In this example, we will add simple business rules to validate the country from the list of countries and check the capital. Right now, don't worry about following the business rules value as it is to let you know that this is where we will write our business rule and use it in a service project.

```
1.    using System;
2.    using System.Collections.Generic;
3.
4.    namespace Microservices.CountryCapital.Domain
5.    {
6.        public class ValidateCountryDomain : IValidateCountryDomain
7.        {
```

```
8.                    List<string> ValidCountries = new List<string>() {
     "UnitesStates", "India", "Russia", "Japan" };

9.

10.                   Dictionary<string, string> ValidateCapitals = new
     Dictionary<string, string>() {

11.                  { "UnitedStates", "Washington" },

12.                  { "India", "NewDelhi" },

13.                  {"Russia","Moscow" },

14.                  {"Japan","Tokyo" }

15.             };

16.


17.         public Boolean Validate(string country)

18.             {

19.                 return ValidCountries.Contains(country);

20.             }

21.

22.         public Boolean ValidateCapital(string capital, string
     country)

23.             {

24.                 return ValidateCapitals[country].Equals(capital);

25.             }

26.

27.         }

28.     }
```

Here the business rules are very trivial and for demonstration purposes only. It will give you an idea of where to write the business rules.

Service project

This project acts as an intermediate between the controllers and subsequent layers. Consider the project as a ViewModel where we call different services and map the relevant data to pass it to the controller. As you can see, the **GetCountryByIdAsync** method is calling the repository to get the data and then validate the response by calling the domain project. If the response is not valid we will be passing **isValid** as false so that controller can handle it and pass the relevant message to the UI.

```
1.    using SM = Microservices.CountryCapital.Services.Models;
```

```csharp
2.   using System.Collections.Generic;
3.   using Microservices.CountryCapital.Infrastructure;
4.   using IM = Microservices.CountryCapital.Infrastructure.Models;
5.   using System.Threading.Tasks;
6.   using Microservices.CountryCapital.Domain;
7.   using System.Linq;
8.
9.   namespace Microservices.CountryCapital.Services
10.  {
11.      public class CountryCapitalService : ICountryCapitalService
12.      {
13.          private IRepository _repository;
14.          private IValidateCountryDomain _validateCountryDomain;
15.              public CountryCapitalService(IRepository repository,
     IValidateCountryDomain validateCountryDomain)
16.          {
17.              _repository = repository;
18.              _validateCountryDomain = validateCountryDomain;
19.          }
20.
21.  public async Task<SM.Country> GetCountryByIdAsync(int countryId)
22.          {
23.                      IM.Country content = await _repository.
     FindCountryByIdAsync(countryId);
24.          SM.Country country = new SM.Country()
25.          {
26.              Capital = content.Capital,
27.              Name=content.Name
28.          };
29.          if (content.isValid())
30.                      country.isValid = _validateCountryDomain.
     Validate(content.Name);
31.              else
32.                  country.isValid = false;
33.
```

```
34.                    return country;
35.              }
36.
37.          public async Task<List<SM.Country>> GetCountriesAsync()
38.          {
39.              List<SM.Country> countries = new List<SM.Country>();
40.              IQueryable<IM.Country> contents = await _repository.
     GetCountriesAsync();
41.              foreach (var item in contents)
42.              {
43.                  countries.Add(new SM.Country()
44.                  {
45.                      Capital = item.Capital,
46.                      Name=item.Name
47.                  });
48.              }
49.
50.              return countries;
51.          }
52.      }
53.  }
```

API Project

This project will contain your application configuration and controller's endpoints exposed to the outside world. As you can notice, we have two GET endpoints. One will return all the countries and the other will accept the country id to return the id-specific details.

```
1.    using System;
2.    using System.Collections.Generic;
3.    using System.Linq;
4.    using System.Threading.Tasks;
5.    using Microservices.CountryCapital.Services;
6.    using Microsoft.AspNetCore.Http;
7.    using Microsoft.AspNetCore.Mvc;
8.
```

```csharp
9.    namespace Microservices.CountryCapital.API.Controllers
10.   {
11.       [Route("api/country")]
12.       public class CountryController : ControllerBase
13.       {
14.           ICountryCapitalService _countryCapitalService;
15.                   public  CountryController(ICountryCapitalService
      countryCapitalService)
16.           {
17.               _countryCapitalService = countryCapitalService;
18.           }
19.
20.           [HttpGet]
21.           public async Task<IActionResult> AllAsync()
22.           {
23.                   var countrylist = await _countryCapitalService.
      GetCountriesAsync();
24.               return Ok(countrylist);
25.           }
26.
27.           [HttpGet("{id}",Name = "GetByCountryId")]
28.           public async Task<IActionResult> GetByCountryId(int id)
29.           {
30.                   var country = await _countryCapitalService.
      GetCountryByIdAsync(id);
31.               if (country.isValid)
32.                   return Ok(country);
33.               else
34.                   return StatusCode(StatusCodes.Status400BadRequest,
      "Not a valid country");
35.           }
36.       }
37.   }
```

Configuring startup

This class will have your application configuration. Under the configure service, you can see we have injected a class for dependency injection. We have injected the S3 repository and the file repository is commented out. As already discussed, if you need a file repository, then you need to uncomment the file repository and comment out the S3 repository. You don't need to make changes at any other place. Also, we have added OpenAPI specifications using swagger.

```
1.    using Microservices.CountryCapital.Domain;

2.    using Microservices.CountryCapital.Infrastructure;

3.    using Microservices.CountryCapital.Services;

4.    using Microsoft.AspNetCore.Builder;

5.    using Microsoft.AspNetCore.Hosting;

6.    using Microsoft.Extensions.Configuration;

7.    using Microsoft.Extensions.DependencyInjection;

8.

9.    namespace Microservices.CountryCapital.API

10.   {

11. 1    public class Startup

12.       {

13.           private bool IsLocalEnvironment = false;

14.

      public Startup(IHostingEnvironment env,IConfiguration configuration)

15.           {

16.               Configuration = configuration;

17.               IsLocalEnvironment = env.IsEnvironment("Local");

18.           }

19.

20.          public static IConfiguration Configuration { get; private
      set; }

21.

22.  2 // This method gets called by the runtime. Use this method to add
      services to the container

23.           public void ConfigureServices(IServiceCollection services)

24.           {

      services.AddMvc();
```

```
25.              services.AddScoped<IRepository,FileRepository>();
26.              //services.AddScoped<IRepository, S3Repository>();
27.    services.AddScoped<ICountryCapitalService,
       CountryCapitalService>();
28.    services.AddScoped<IValidateCountryDomain,
       ValidateCountryDomain>();
29.              services.AddSwaggerGen();
     }
30.
31.        // This method gets called by the runtime. Use this method
       to configure the HTTP request pipeline
32.              public  void  Configure(IApplicationBuilder  app,
       IHostingEnvironment env)
33.        {
34.            app.UseSwagger();
35.            app.UseSwaggerUI(c =>
36.            {
37.                if (IsLocalEnvironment)
38.                    c.SwaggerEndpoint("/swagger/v1/swagger.json",
       "CountryCapitalService V1");
39.                else
40.                    c.SwaggerEndpoint("/countrycapital/swagger/v1/
       swagger.json", "CountryCapitalService V1");
41.
42.                c.RoutePrefix = string.Empty;
43.            });
44.
45.            if (env.IsDevelopment())
46.            {
47.                app.UseDeveloperExceptionPage();
48.            }
49.            else
50.            {
51.                app.UseHsts();
52.            }
```

```
53.
54.                    app.UseMvc();
55.            }
56.        }
57.    }
```

Inject environment and configuration in runtime. Based on the environment, we will decide whether the code runs locally or not.

Register different classes inside the .NET Core dependency injection container.

There are three ways to inject service with different lifetimes:

a) **AddSingleton()**: Creates a single instance of the service.

b) **AddScoped()** : Every **HttpRequest** gets new instance. One object within a scope of **HttpRequest**.

c) **AddTransient()**: Everytime new instance gets created irrespective of the scope of the same **HttpRequest** or different.

Here, we inject the **Repository** class to be used by the application as discussed earlier.

Configure OpenAPI specification using swagger.

Serverless template

A serverless template is useful when you need to deploy the Lambda function in AWS.

A brief description of the cloud formation template is as follows:

1. Configure API gateway which will map the Lambda function as a proxy and forward the incoming requests to it.

2. The handler property in JSON will have the Lambda function full path.

3. Memory size and timeout can be configurable. The maximum timeout is 15 minutes, and the maximum memory size is 3008 MB.

4. The role needs to be configured which we have created in the previous section.

5. **CodeUri** property is empty and is used by AWS to locate the code after it is deployed. When you deploy the Lambda function, it gets compiled, bundles up, and deployed in the S3 bucket. The codeuri property of the serverless template helps AWS to locate the deployed code at the time of deployment.

Once deployed, you can also check the deployment status in the AWS cloud formation service. If you want to delete the Lambda function manually, it is safe to delete it from the cloud formation stack which will delete all the dependent resources automatically.

```
1.    {
2.        "AWSTemplateFormatVersion" : "2010-09-09",
3.        "Transform" : "AWS::Serverless-2016-10-31",
4.        "Description" : "Template for CountryCapital",
5.        "Parameters": {
6.        },
   "Globals": {
7.            "Api": {
8.                "EndpointConfiguration" : "REGIONAL",
9.                "Cors"                 : {
10.                    "AllowMethods" : "'*,DELETE, GET, HEAD, OPTIONS,
       PATCH, POST, PUT'",
11.                    "AllowHeaders" : "'*,Content-Type,X-Amz-
       Date,Authorization,X-Api-Key,X-Amz-Security-Token,access-control-
       allow-credentials,access-control-allow-origin,x-orgid,x-c-
       oachid,x-playerid,x-coachid,x-tournyid,observe,Access-Control-
       Allow-Origin'",
12.                    "AllowOrigin"   : "'*'"
13.                },
14.                "Name": "Microservices.CountryCapital"
15.
16.            }
17.        },
18.        "Resources": {
19.          "DefaultFunction" : {
20.            "Type" : "AWS::Serverless::Function",
21.            "Properties": {
22.            "Handler": "Microservices.CountryCapital.API::Microservices.
       CountryCapital.API.LambdaEntryPoint::FunctionHandlerAsync",
23.                "FunctionName" : "CountryCapitalServerlessApi",
24.                "Runtime": "dotnetcore3.1",
25.                "CodeUri": "",
```

```
26.                "Description": "CountryCapital API",
27.                "MemorySize": 256,
28.                "Timeout": 30,
29.                 "Role":  "arn:aws:iam::829136968147:role/lambda_execute_
       role",
30.                "Policies": [ "AWSLambdaFullAccess" ],
31.        "Events"       : {
32.                        "PutResource": {
33.                            "Type": "Api",
34.                            "Properties": {
35.                                "Path" : "/{proxy+}",
36.                                "Method": "ANY"
37.                            }
38.                        }
39.                }
40.            }
41.        }
42.    },
43.    "Outputs": {
44.    }
45. }
```

Get custom domain

Nowadays, there are a lot of sites from where you can get a free domain. we will use *freenom.com* to register our domain. You can easily get a domain from here and I will help you to get one of those.

1. Login into the freenom website

2. Under service -> Register New Domain

The following diagram shows how to register a new domain in freenom:

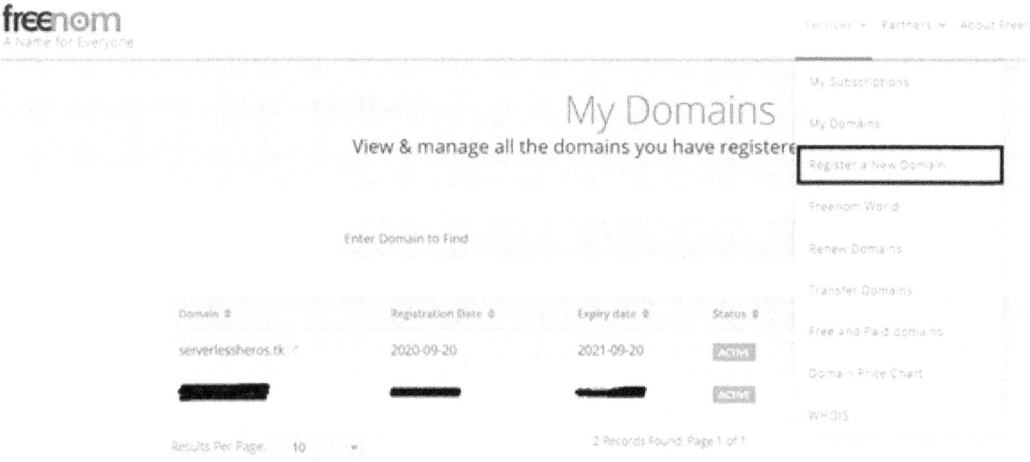

Figure 5.4: Freenom Domain Registration

3. Now search for the domain of your choice. In my case, I searched for **serverlessheros** domain and choose **tk** (following screenshot).

Figure 5.5: Search Domain

> Note: I have already used the heroserverless domain and so you might need to search for some unique domain that will be available for your application.

Create a self-signed certificate

In the coming steps, we will register countrycapital Lambda to the API gateway. To configure the API gateway, you need an SSL certificate. However, for tests or tutorial purposes, you don't need to buy SSL from CA (which is quite expensive). Here, we will use OpenSSL to generate our self-signed certificate. The steps are as follows:

1. For OpenSSL installation in the different operating system refer to the following table:

Operating System	Command
Mac	`brew install openssl`
Linux	`apt-get install openssl`
Windows	Need to download MSI from the openssl site

Table 5.1

2. Follow these commands step-by-step:

   a. `openssl genrsa -des3 -passout pass:x -out server.pass.key 2048`

   b. `openssl rsa -passin pass:x -in server.pass.key -out server.key`

   c. `rm server.pass.key`

   d. `openssl req -new -key server.key -out server.csr`

      • Country – US

      • State or Province Name – California

      • Common name - *.**serverlessheros.tk** (in your case, whichever domain you chose from freenom in the previous step, use that domain here. Make sure to put * (wildcard) before the domain name)

   e. `openssl x509 -req -sha256 -days 365 -in server.csr -signkey server.key -out server.crt`

Add a certificate to AWS Certificate Manager

Now, it's time to use the certificate you have generated in AWS. Go to AWS console and then to Certificate Manager. Select the import certificate option. Now, open the **server.crt** (generated in the previous section) in Notepad, and copy the content to the certificate body. Similarly, open the **server.key** in Notepad, and copy the content to the certificate private key.

The following screenshot shows AWS Certificate Manager to import the certificate:

Figure 5.6: *AWS Certificate Manager*

Configure API gateway

Now, we will configure the API gateway which acts as a reverse proxy to the Lambda function which we have deployed. Go to the AWS console and then click on API gateway. There, you need to go to the custom domain section and click on **Create**. Fill in the domain name as **API.serverlessheros.tk** (prefix API in front of your domain name to identify this as an endpoint in your application). Select the certificate from **Certificate Manager** and finally click **Create** domain name.

The following screenshot shows how to register a new domain in API gateway:

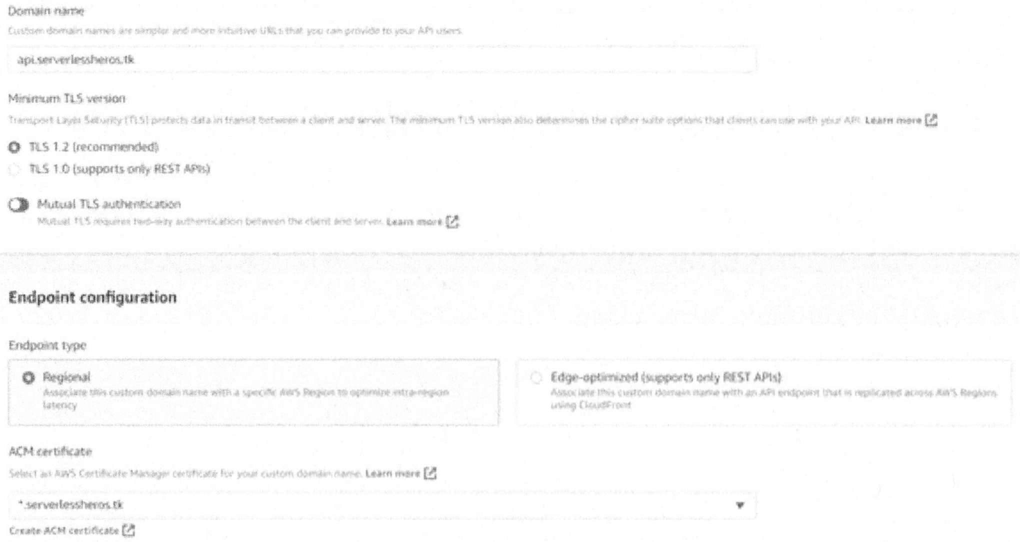

Figure 5.7: *API Gateway Domain Registration*

Deploy Lambda Function

Now you can deploy the Lambda function from Visual studio (deploying from the visual studio is not an ideal way for deployment. We will discuss the deployment strategies in the upcoming chapters). Right-click on the API project and select **Publish to AWS Lambda**.

The following screenshot shows an option in Visual Studio to deploy a serverless application:

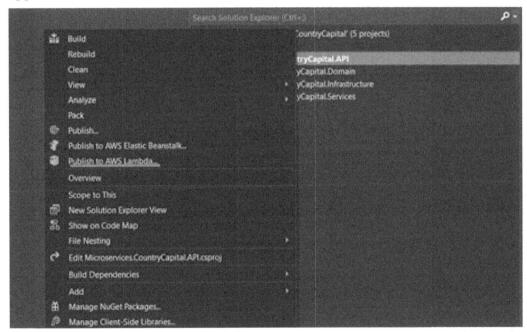

Figure 5.8: Publish AWS Lambda

Make sure you select the correct profile and region. Give the stack name and select an S3 bucket from the selected region. Click **Publish** and it will create a Lambda function and map it to the API gateway.

The following screenshot shows the serverless application deployment configuration:

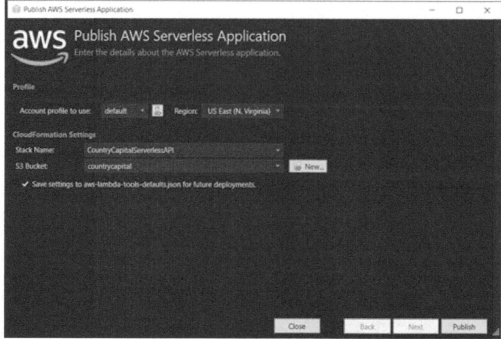

Figure 5.9: Lambda Deployment configuration

Now, to check whether everything is properly deployed or not, go to Lambda service. The following screenshot shows the AWS Lambda section where you can see your deployed Lambda application.

Figure 5.10: AWS Lambda Functions

Go to the API gateway and navigate through the APIs section to see if it got integrated with the Lambda function.

The following screenshot shows the API gateway configured after deployment:

Figure 5.11: AWS API Gateway APIs

The following screenshot shows the Lambda configuration in the API gateway:

Figure 5.12: *Lambda Configuration in API Gateway*

Configure Route 53

Finally, configure Route 53. To configure Route 53, we must create a hosted zone. The following screenshot shows AWS Route 53 hosted zone settings:

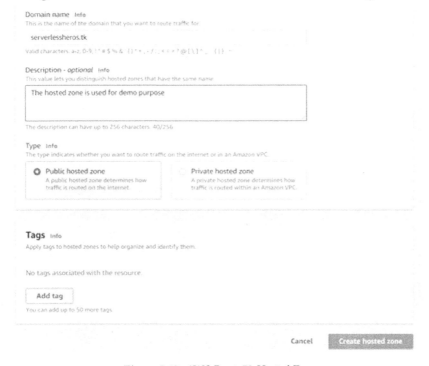

Figure 5.13: *AWS Route53 Hosted Zone*

After the hosted zone is created, we need to follow these steps:

1. Map the nameserver (NS record) from the API gateway hosted zone to freenom custom nameservers settings (wherever you create your domain).

The following screenshot shows how to map AWS Route 53 nameservers to freenom custom nameservers:

Figure 5.14: Freenom Custom Nameservers

2. Map the API gateway to this hosted zone so that the request with the URL with **api.serverlessheros.tk** will be forwarded to it.

The following screenshot shows how to configure the API Gateway endpoint in Route 53 by creating a record:

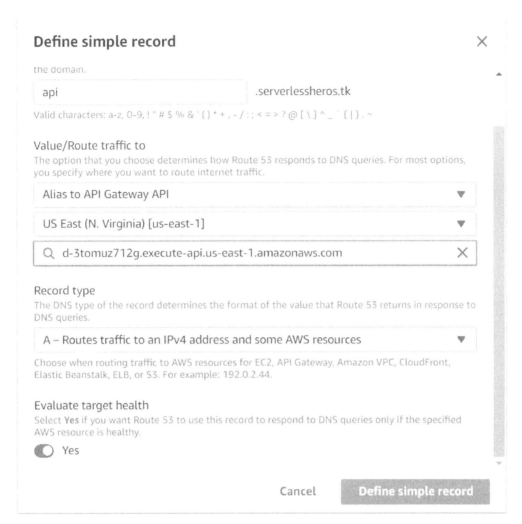

Figure 5.15: *Route 53 A Record for API Gateway*

Final step

The last step of this tutorial is to check if everything is configured properly. Type **https://api.serverlessheros.tk/countrycapital/index.html** in the browser and it will open the API endpoint configured in your startup project.

The following screenshot shows the OpenAPI specification of a serverless application after deployment to AWS Lambda:

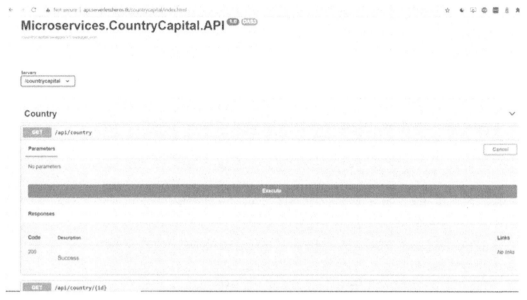

Figure 5.16: Swagger API

> You can download the preceding code from my Github account https://github.com/sarkarstanmoy/AWS-Microservices/tree/master/Chapter5/Microservices.CountryCapital.

Conclusion

In this chapter, we saw how to configure different AWS services, custom domains, and AWS certificates to create a serverless web API cost-effectively. Remember microservice is not the silver bullet and often puts challenges that might add complexity and operational burden to your system. Microservices are useful for big applications. For small applications, consider monolithic initially. Don't try to design every system with microservices which can be an overburden for your team. Plan diligently and decide whether you need microservices. In the next chapter, we will discuss different communication patterns between microservices.

Points to remember

- Domain project is where you will define your business logic and is the heart of the application. Ideally, the domain should be independent and doesn't reference any project.

- The infrastructure layer of the project will have data persistence logic using ORMs and other infrastructure-related implementation, like SQS, logging.

- Repository pattern helps to abstract the underlying implementation of data retrieval.

- AWS Certificate Manager is a centralized repository where you can import your custom certificate and use it across services.

- API gateway acts as a reverse proxy for Lambda.

- To host your domain in Route 53, you need to create a hosted zone.

- A swagger is a tool that follows OpenAPI specification standards.

Multiple choice questions

1. **Which layer should be independent and contains business logic?**
    a. Domain
    b. Infrastructure
    c. Presentation

2. **API gateway acts as a _____ for AWS Lambda**
    a. Forward proxy
    b. Reverse proxy
    c. Server

3. **To host a domain in Route 53, we first need to create _____?**
    a. Hosted zone
    b. Hosted area
    c. Name server

Answer

1. a
2. b
3. a

CHAPTER 6

Communication Patterns and Service Discovery

Communication works for those who work at it.

--- John Powell

Introduction

The preceding quote is relevant for this chapter because here we will discuss microservice communication strategies. Software systems communicate with each other either synchronously or asynchronously. In synchronous communication, the calling system must wait for the response from the source system before further processing. In the case of asynchronous communication, the calling system sends a request and doesn't wait for the response to the process.

In the microservice software paradigm, communication can either be synchronous or asynchronous. In the previous chapter, we developed an application to retrieve the country and its respective capital using Lambda. We hosted the application using the API gateway and Route 53. Usually, the request/response pattern in Web API is synchronous where the client expects data in real-time. Synchronous communication degrades the performance and speed of the overall system. In this chapter, we will discuss how to make microservice communication asynchronous by using AWS EventBridge. AWS EventBridge is an event-driven system that consists of publishers and subscribers. It works on the pub/sub model where the subscribers consume events published by a publisher in the event channel.

Microservices need to collaborate to process incoming requests. However, microservice first needs to locate other microservice to start communication. For this, we can use the service discovery using AWS Cloud Map. The Cloud Map provides a service registry that enables microservices to locate each other. It helps to reduce failure in case of endpoint changes. For example, if one microservice endpoint gets changed or the version gets updated, then all the microservices calling it will also be affected, leading to system failure. With AWS Cloud Map, it is the centralized location where each microservice locates another microservice before initiating any communication. Any update in the microservice endpoint only requires changes in the service map without affecting any other part of the system.

Structure

In this chapter, we will discuss the following topics:

- Communication patterns
  - o Point-to-point
    - Fire-and-Forget
    - Request/reply
  - o Publish/subscribe
    - Fire-and-Forget
    - Request/reply
  - o Asynchronous Lambda invocation
    - EventBridge
    - API gateway integration
  - o Service discovery
    - AWS Cloud Map

Objective

In this chapter, we will learn about different microservice communication patterns and the services available in AWS to achieve them. We will also discuss AWS EventBridge and how to improve the performance of the application. We will also, discuss the AWS Cloud Map and when to use it. By the end of this chapter, you will have a good idea about the AWS EventBridge, queues, topics, AWS Cloud Map, and where to use it.

Communication patterns

One of the important aspects of microservice architecture is communication. How should microservices communicate with each other? How the external system will interact with microservices? Should they use synchronous or asynchronous communication? In the subsequent topics, we will discuss some important communication patterns.

Point-to-point

In **point-to-point (p2p)** communication, the producer (sender) exchanges messages with the consumer (receiver) using message queues. Queues ensure that only one receiver can consume a given message, although you can connect multiple consumers to the queue. The main advantage of this pattern is the horizontal scaling at the receiver's end. The number of receivers processing the messages can scale in and scale-out according to the load. Also, from the consumer side, queue helps flatten peak loads of messages and prevent the receiver from flooding, eventually buying time for the receiver to scale. You can further attach a **dead-letter queue (DLQ)** to SQS to store unprocessed messages.

Fire-and-Forget

Here, the sender does not expect any response from the receiver and it will forget about the message one sends to the queue.

The following diagram shows the sender sending a message to the queue without expecting any response:

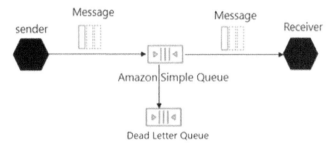

Figure 6.1: Point to point one-way communication

Request/reply

The sender will send a message to the receiver in one queue and wait for the response from another queue. The message sent by the sender does have more information other than payloads like the response queue where the response needs to send the correlation token.

The following diagram shows the sender sending a message through one queue and expecting a response from another queue:

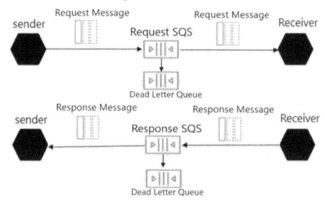

Figure 6.2: Point to point two-way communication

Publish/subscribe

A publish/subscribe communication model is usually implemented using topics. Here, the sender sends messages to topics and it gets broadcasted to the subscribers (usually more than one) asynchronously. In AWS, you can attach DLQ to the SNS topic which will store messages that are not successfully delivered to the subscribers.

Fire-and-Forget

Here, the sender does not expect any response from the receiver and it will forget about the message one sends to the topic.

The following diagram shows the sender sending a message to the queue without expecting any response:

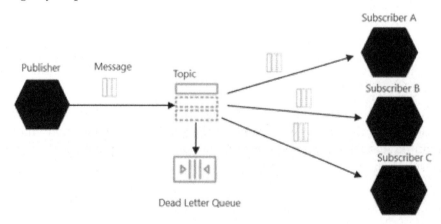

Figure 6.3: Publish-Subscribe one-way communication

Request/reply

The sender will send a message to the receiver on the topic and wait for the response from the queue. The message sent by the sender also sends additional information other than the payload like the response queue where the response needs to send the correlation token.

The following diagram shows the sender publishing message using the topic and getting a response from the queue:

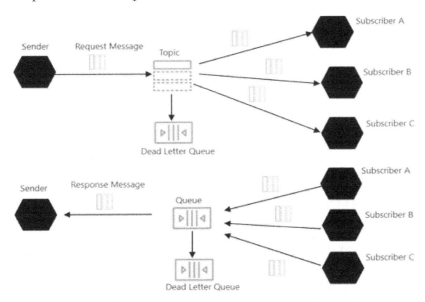

Figure 6.4: *Publish-Subscribe two-way communication*

Asynchronous Lambda invocation

In the previous chapter, we configured the Lambda endpoint with the API gateway which resulted in synchronous communication. The API gateway will wait for Lambda to respond, and eventually, pass the response to downstream systems. Suppose in case of an ordering system, where Lambda makes a call to other microservices to update inventory and initiate a payment, in that case, it must wait for all these microservices to complete. In some cases, if any one of the microservice fails to respond, the message gets lost, which eventually leads to a failed transaction.

The following diagram shows the complexity involved when Lambdas communicate directly with each other:

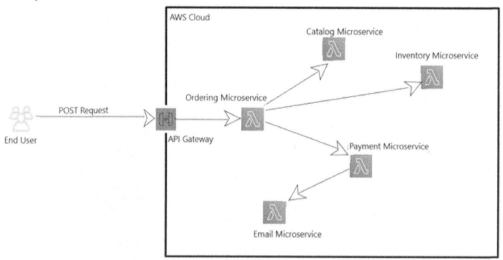

Figure 6.5: Microservices direct communication

EventBridge

EventBridge comes to the rescue for the preceding problem. As per AWS, "Amazon EventBridge is a serverless event bus that makes it easy to connect applications using data from your applications, **Software-as-a-Service (SaaS)** applications, and AWS services". In the EventBridge, you can write rules based on the payload property which will redirect the messages to destinations like Lambda and step function. Also, you can schedule the execution of Lambda, step function, and other AWS services.

The following figure shows the EventBridge interaction with other AWS services:

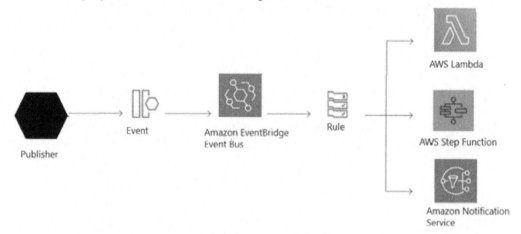

Figure 6.6: AWS Event Bridge

API gateway integration

Integrating AWS EventBridge with the API gateway can make the post/put request asynchronous and improve the performance of the application. Let us understand this with an example:

- Suppose your application supports a payment feature integrating with the 3rd party payment system. Rather than directly calling payment microservice from your external client and waiting for the response, it is better to publish the request message in a messaging system like a queue, topic, or EventBridge, and return 202 status code with a status endpoint to the downstream system. The payment microservice will react to the event published and initiate the payment process. Once the payment is complete, the response will be published to the messaging system, and the downstream system will get a success message from the status endpoint. In this way, your application will not have to wait for the payment microservice to complete making it an asynchronous transaction.

The following diagram shows the communication flow when frontend application requests post for the event-driven system. In this way, your frontend application will not have to wait for the payment API to complete:

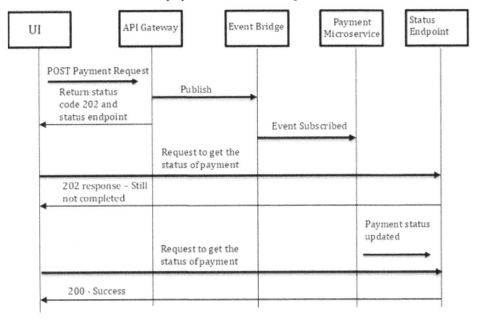

Figure 6.7: Event-driven flow for the POST message

The following diagram shows how the events from EventBridge can trigger other respective microservice based on a rule. Here, the ordering system publishes the message in EventBridge. Other microservices subscribe to the respective message and start processing the request. Once the payment microservice completes the transaction, it will publish a message to queue for email microservice to send an email to the user:

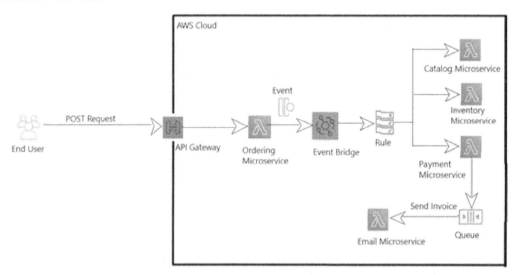

Figure 6.8: *Event-driven design using Event Bridge*

The underlying diagram shows another design scenario where the request message is redirected to the step function. The advantage of using the step function is it will coordinate among microservices and handle the error gracefully. The ordering system's only responsibility is to publish the message in EventBridge and the rest is taken care of by the step function. The next chapter will discuss how to configure the step function and coordinate with microservices.

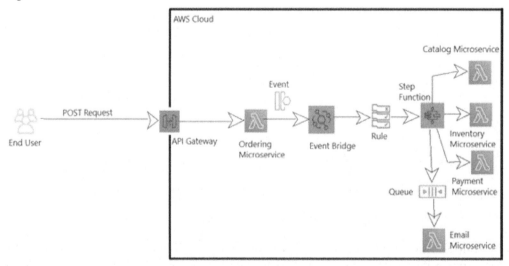

Figure 6.9: *Event-driven design using Event Bridge and step function*

Service discovery

As we have discussed service discovery in *Chapter 4: Microservices patterns,* it states that it is used to register microservice addresses for intra communication. If one microservice wants to communicate with another microservice, it will first refer to the service discovery registry to get the address for communication. It is very much like a telephone directory. AWS provides Cloud Map service to achieve service discovery.

AWS Cloud Map

According to AWS, *"Cloud Map allows you to register any application resources, such as databases, queues, microservices, and other cloud resources, with custom names."* The advantage of a Cloud Map in your application is you can change the address of any service without redeploying the application. Also, the Cloud Map monitors the registered services and returns the up-to-date addresses. This will eventually increase productivity as the team doesn't need to spend time tracking and updating service endpoints.

The following diagram shows microservice discovery using the AWS Cloud Map. **Microservice A** is requesting the AWS Cloud Map to share the latest endpoint of **microservice B** and then it will start sending a request to **microservice B:**

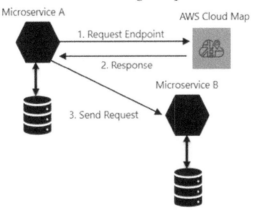

Figure 6.10: Microservice service discovery flow

Conclusion

In this chapter, we discussed different messaging patterns you should keep in your toolbox while designing microservices. We witnessed how EventBridge acts as a mediator between the API gateway and microservices to increase the performance of the system. Similarly, queues and topics help to increase the resiliency of the system, making it loosely coupled and helps to avoid a single point of failure. Cloud Map is another AWS service that you can use to register microservices. New microservice can use Cloud Map to register itself and refer to communicate to other microservices. Cloud Map can also be used to store database connections, application settings, and so on. In the next chapter, we will develop an application using the messaging tools which we discussed in this chapter.

Points to remember

- Queue helps flatten peak loads of messages and prevent the receiver from flooding eventually.

- In Fire-and-Forget, the sender doesn't expect any response from the receiver.

- In publish/subscribe, the sender will send messages to topics and it gets broadcasted to the subscribers.

- Amazon EventBridge is a serverless event bus that makes it easy to connect applications using data from your applications, like **Software-as-a-Service (SaaS)** applications.

- In EventBridge, you can write rules based on the payload property which will redirect the messages to destinations like Lambda and step functions.

- Service discovery is used when one microservice wants to communicate with another microservice.

- Cloud Map allows you to register any application resources, such as databases, queues, microservices, and other cloud resources, with custom names.

Multiple choice questions

1. **What are the messaging tools?**
   a. Queue
   b. Topics
   c. Event Bus
   d. All of the above

2. **In the Fire-and-Forget messaging pattern, the source doesn't expect a response from the destination.**
   a. True
   b. False

3. ___ is used to store unprocessed messages.

   a. Queues

   b. Dead-letter queues

   c. Topics

4. In ___, different parts of the application are reacted to events.

   a. Event-driven application

   b. Domain-driven application

   c. None of the above

5. ___ is an AWS service that registers application resources.

   a. S3

   b. Load balancer

   c. Cloud Map

   d. None of the above

6. What does 202 status indicate?

   a. Request denied

   b. Not found

   c. Request accepted

   d. None of the above

Answer

1. d
2. a
3. b
4. a
5. c
6. c

CHAPTER 7

Collaborating Between Microservices

Write programs that do one thing and do it well. Write programs to work together.

--- Douglas Mcllroy – Mathematician, engineer, programmer

Introduction

Microservices collaborate among themselves either using synchronous or asynchronous communication. These collaborations are necessary for a distributed, loosely coupled system because when changes occur within the system, they need to be reconciled in different parts of it. For client-server interaction, most of the time, synchronous communication (HTTP protocol) is preferred to fetch the results immediately with API gateway as the proxy. However, for internal microservice communication within the system, that is, among microservices, asynchronous event-driven communication is preferred. An event is a signal that something has changed within the system. If any other part of the system is interested in this change, it will subscribe to the event from the message broker. Message brokers like RabbitMQ, Azure Service Bus, AWS Topic, and AWS EventBridge can be used. The source microservice will publish the message (which consists of custom headers) into the event bus and based on some rules, the message will be subscribed or routed to the destination microservice.

In this chapter, we will implement an asynchronous event-driven system using AWS serverless application and EventBridge. EventBridge is a serverless event bus that connects a wide variety of AWS services using events. Here, you will learn how to use EventBridge efficiently and route the message among microservices.

Structure

- Event-driven design prerequisite
- AWS step function
  - Setup
    - Step function tasks
    - State machine
    - Serverless template
- EventBridge
  - Create event bus
  - Create rule
    - Configure patterns
    - Configure targets
- Connecting microservices
  - Configuring API gateway
    - Create resource
    - Create method
    - Configure headers
    - Configure mapping template
    - Add method response
    - Deploy and test

Objective

In this chapter, you will learn how to publish a message from the API gateway to the EventBridge, how to create EventBridge rules to route messages, and how to integrate it with the step function. You will also learn to create a step function from scratch and how to use and deploy it in AWS.

At the end of this chapter, you will be efficient enough to create your step function and integrate it with the EventBridge to create a loosely coupled system.

Event-driven design prerequisite

Event-driven architecture is not the solution to all the problems that exist in the real world. One of the challenges in this architecture is to monitor and maintain the system. However, it gains popularity because of its loosely coupled nature and resiliency. When you design an event-driven system, it is good to start with event storming. Event storming is a workshop-based method where persons from different areas, like developers, domain experts, business analysts, etc. collaborate and figure out what is going on within different domains involved in the system. It helps you to identify the bounded context and how these bounded contexts communicate using events that eventually lead to microservices.

In the upcoming section of this chapter, we will simulate an order processing system where the user will initiate order requests and AWS will process the order. We will discuss in detail each part of the application one by one and finally connect them all.

AWS step function

AWS step function is used to orchestrate serverless functions into business-critical operations. State machines are built using **Amazon States Language**, which is JSON-structured to represent the elements. AWS step function connects and coordinates different independent, language-agnostic serverless applications. For users, it provides a flow chart visualization to map the information flow. AWS step function also handles the exception and has a retry mechanism.

To start building our pragmatic order processing application, we will first discuss the **OrderProcessor** step function.

Setup

Since this book is focused on .NET Core 3.1 application, we will create a step function project using Visual Studio 2019. We create an **OrderProcessor** step function.

The following screenshot represents the selection of AWS serverless application template to create a serverless application:

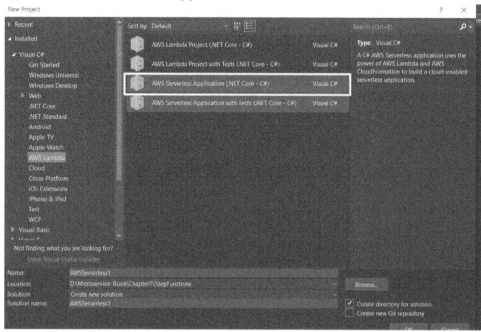

Figure 7.1: AWS Lambda Project

The following screenshot shows Lambda blueprints. We will select the step functions:

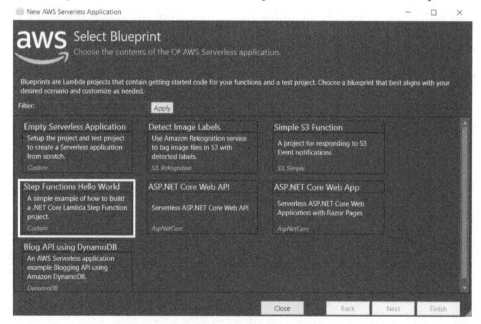

Figure 7.2: Lambda Blueprints

Once the step function project is generated, different configuration files get created which we will discuss here:

Step function tasks

Step function provides a way to coordinate between the serverless functions through the state. Each state performs a specific task, and once performed, the step function will execute the subsequent state. States are the individual building block of step function which contain business logic to perform.

The following sample code is the processOrder state which simulates order processing business logic and logs information in the CloudWatch. Each state will create a Lambda function where you can inject your business logic to execute. Here, the **processOrder** state will create the **processOrder** Lambda function:

```
1.    public State ProcessOrder(OrderEvent order, ILambdaContext context)
2.            {
3.              Console.WriteLine("OrderProcessing Started");
4.                    Console.Write(Newtonsoft.Json.JsonConvert.
       SerializeObject(order));
5.              return new State()
6.              {
7.                 OrderId=order.detail.orderId,
8.                 Message=" Process Order completed successfully"
9.              };
10.          }
```

State machine

To coordinate between the states, we need a state machine where we can design our flow of execution.

The following screenshot shows the state machine having **OrderProcessor**, **EmailProcessor**, and **PaymentProcessor** tasks which are coordinated by step function state machine to achieve a business functionality:

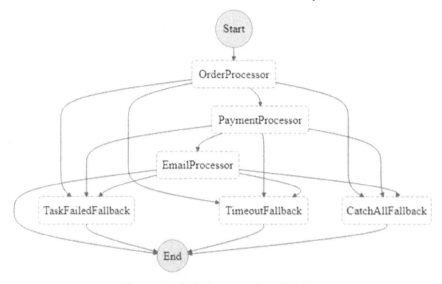

Figure 7.3: OrderProcessor State Machine

To generate the state machine, we will use Amazon States Language, as shown in the following screenshot. Let's go through some of its details:

Amazon States Language JSON starts with a comment that will define what this state machine does. Each state machine can have multiple states with its type. There are different types of states:

- **Pass**: A passing state passes its input to output without performing any tasks.
- **Task**: Runs the serverless functions.
- **Choice**: Choice is like the if/else condition.
- **Wait**: Pauses the state machine.
- **Succeed**: End of the state machine successfully.
- **Fail**: End of the state machine unsuccessfully.
- **Parallel**: Runs multiple state machines parallelly.

```
1.  {
2.      "Comment": "State Machine",
3.      "StartAt": "OrderProcessor",
4.      "States": {
```

```
5.              "OrderProcessor": {
6.                "Type": "Task",
7.                "Resource": "${OrderProcessorTask.Arn}",
8.                "TimeoutSeconds": 300,
9.                "Retry": [
10.                  {
11.                      "ErrorEquals": [ "Lambda.ServiceException",
      "Lambda.SdkClientException", "Lambda.Unknown" ],
12.                    "IntervalSeconds": 1,
13.                    "MaxAttempts": 2,
14.                    "BackoffRate": 2.0
15.                  }
16.                ],
17.                "Catch": [
18.                  {
19.                    "ErrorEquals": [ "States.TaskFailed" ],
20.                    "Next": "TaskFailedFallback"
21.                  },
22.                  {
23.                    "ErrorEquals": [ "States.Timeout" ],
24.                    "Next": "TimeoutFallback"
25.                  },
26.                  {
27.                    "ErrorEquals": [ "States.ALL" ],
28.                    "Next": "CatchAllFallback"
29.                  }
30.                ],
31.                "Next": "PaymentProcessor"
32.              },
```

The state machine starts with the **OrderProcessor** state defined in the **StartAt** property. Here, it is defined under the state property, that is a JSON collection, to define the number of states used in the step function. This state is of the Task type to run the serverless function. As you have noticed, the **Resource** property's value is **OrderProcessorTask.Arn,** which is the Amazon Resource Name for OrderProcessor Lambda defined in the serverless template (will be discussed in the next section). The **TimeoutSeconds** is the time interval of Lambda execution after which it will stop processing if the execution takes more than 5 minutes. You can change the time interval to a maximum of 15 minutes. The Retry property is used to retry the execution in case of failures, like **ServiceException**, **SdkClientException** mentioned in the **ErrorEquals** property. You can change the number of retries in the **MaxAttempts** property. The **Catch** block will catch the exception and handle it in subsequent steps. In this case, the **TaskFailedFallback** state is of the type Fail, which ends the step function unsuccessfully. Finally, **Next** will determine the next step to execute after successful execution.

```
1.          "PaymentProcessor": {
2.            "Type": "Task",
3.            "Resource": "${PaymentProcessorTask.Arn}",
4.            "TimeoutSeconds": 300,
5.            "Retry": [
6.              {
7.                "ErrorEquals": [ "Lambda.ServiceException", "Lambda.
      SdkClientException", "Lambda.Unknown" ],
8.                "IntervalSeconds": 1,
9.                "MaxAttempts": 2,
10.               "BackoffRate": 2.0
11.             }
12.           ],
13.           "Catch": [
14.             {
15.               "ErrorEquals": [ "States.TaskFailed" ],
16.               "Next": "TaskFailedFallback"
17.             },
18.             {
19.               "ErrorEquals": [ "States.Timeout" ],
20.               "Next": "TimeoutFallback"
21.             },
22.             {
23.               "ErrorEquals": [ "States.ALL" ],
24.               "Next": "CatchAllFallback"
25.             }
26.           ],
```

```
27.                 "Next": "EmailProcessor"
28.             },
29.         "EmailProcessor": {
30.             "Type": "Task",
31.             "Resource": "${EmailProcessorTask.Arn}",
32.             "TimeoutSeconds": 300,
33.             "Retry": [
34.                 {
35.                     "ErrorEquals": [ "Lambda.ServiceException", "Lambda.
    SdkClientException", "Lambda.Unknown" ],
36.                     "IntervalSeconds": 1,
37.                     "MaxAttempts": 2,
38.                     "BackoffRate": 2.0
39.                 }
40.             ],
41.         "Catch": [
42.                 {
43.                     "ErrorEquals": [ "States.TaskFailed" ],
44.                     "Next": "TaskFailedFallback"
45.                 },
46.                 {
47.                     "ErrorEquals": [ "States.Timeout" ],
48.                     "Next": "TimeoutFallback"
49.                 },
50.                 {
51.                     "ErrorEquals": [ "States.ALL" ],
52.                     "Next": "CatchAllFallback"
53.                 }
54.             ],
55.         "End": true
56.         },
```

PaymentProcessor and **EmailProcessor** are the subsequent states of this step functions that will execute. All the configurations of these steps are the same as discussed previously, except the **End** property. The **End** property is used to end the state machine successfully.

```
1.    "TaskFailedFallback": {
2.          "Type": "Fail",
3.          "Cause": "Invalid response.",
4.          "Error": "Task failed due to error occur in the state."
5.        },
6.        "TimeoutFallback": {
7.          "Type": "Fail",
8.          "Cause": "Execution might have stuck somewhere.",
9.          "Error": "State fail due to timeout error."
10.       },
11.       "CatchAllFallback": {
12.         "Type": "Fail",
13.         "Cause": "Invalid response.",
14.         "Error": "Something went wrong as this is caught in states.
     All state fail."
15.       }
16.     }
17.   }
```

TaskFailedFallback, **TimeoutFallback**, and **CatchAllFallback** are the states to handle exceptions and log messages in CloudWatch. **CatchAllFallback** is like a global exception handler that will handle all the unmatched exceptions.

Serverless template

AWS **Serverless Application Model (SAM)** is used to define the serverless function. SAM template contains the configuration data of your serverless function, like the application runtime, serverless timeout, memory size, and so on. It is an extension of CloudFormation which creates and configures a serverless application. The following SAM template is used to configure the step function. As you can notice, we will define the Lambda function under Resources, for example, **OrderProcessorTask,** and will use the function **Amazon Resource Name (ARN)** in the preceding state machine configuration. Each resource in the SAM template will execute as a separate Lambda function running specific business logic defined.

```
1.   {
2.        "AWSTemplateFormatVersion" : "2010-09-09",
3.        "Transform"                : "AWS::Serverless-2016-10-31",
4.        "Description": "An AWS Serverless Application.",
```

```
5.          "Resources": {
6.              "OrderProcessorTask": {
7.                  "Type" : "AWS::Lambda::Function",
8.                  "Properties": {
9.                      "Handler"  : "OrderProcessor::OrderProcessor.
    StepFunctionTasks::ProcessOrder",
10.                     "Role"     : "<<Lambda Role>>",
11.                     "Runtime" : "dotnetcore3.1",
12.                     "MemorySize": 256,
13.                     "Timeout": 30,
14.          "FunctionName" : "OrderProcessor",
15.                     "Code"        : {
16.                         "S3Bucket" : "",
17.                         "S3Key"      : ""
18.                     },
19.                     "Environment": {
20.                         "Variables": {
21.                             "LambdaEnvironment": "dev"
22.                         }
23.                     }
24.                 }
25.             },
```

The SAM template starts with AWSTemplateFormatVersion and Transform properties. The value of these properties is constant and does not modify it. You can then add what your Lambda function does under the **Description** property. **OrderProcessorTask** is a serverless function that has Type as **AWS::Lambda::Function**. You can configure this serverless function by defining its properties, like role, runtime, memory size, etc.

```
1.              "PaymentProcessorTask" : {
2.              "Type" : "AWS::Lambda::Function",
3.              "Properties": {
4.                  "Handler"  : "OrderProcessor::OrderProcessor.
    StepFunctionTasks::ProcessPayment",
5.                  "Role"     : "<<Lambda Role>>",
6.                  "Runtime" : "dotnetcore3.1",
```

```
7.                    "MemorySize": 256,
8.                    "Timeout": 30,
9.        "FunctionName" : "PaymentProcessor",
10.                   "Code"        : {
11.                     "S3Bucket" : "",
12.                     "S3Key"     : ""
13.                   },
14.                   "Environment": {
15.                     "Variables": {
16.                        "LambdaEnvironment": "dev"
17.                     }
18.                   }
19.               }
20.           },
21.
22.     "EmailProcessorTask": {
23.               "Type" : "AWS::Lambda::Function",
24.               "Properties": {
25.                    "Handler" : "OrderProcessor::OrderProcessor.
       StepFunctionTasks::ProcessEmail",
26.                   "Role"     : "<<Lambda Role>>",
27.                   "Runtime" : "dotnetcore3.1",
28.                   "MemorySize": 256,
29.                   "Timeout": 30,
30.        "FunctionName" : "EmailProcessor",
31.                   "Code"        : {
32.                     "S3Bucket" : "",
33.                     "S3Key"     : ""
34.                   },
35.                   "Environment": {
36.                     "Variables": {
37.                        "LambdaEnvironment": "dev"
38.                     }
39.                   }
```

```
40.                   }
41.                },
```

PaymentProcessorTask and **EmailProcessorTask** are defined additional serverless functions that get deployed in the following SAM template:

```
1.     "StateMachine"  : {
2.               "Type" : "AWS::StepFunctions::StateMachine",
3.               "Properties": {
4.                   "RoleArn" : "<<StepFunction Role>>",
5.                   "DefinitionString" : {
6.                       "Fn::Sub" : ""
7.                   },
8.                   "StateMachineName" : "OrderProcessor",
9.                   "LoggingConfiguration": {
10.                  "Level": "ALL",
11.                  "IncludeExecutionData" : true,
12.                      "Destinations": [{"CloudWatchLogsLogGroup":
       "arn:aws:logs:us-east-1:829136968147:log-group:/aws/vendedlogs/
       states/OrderProcessor-Logs:*"}]
13.       }
14.               }
15.           }
16.       },
17.       "Outputs"               : {
18.       }
19.   }
```

StateMachine property is used to define the **StateMachine** configuration. This is different from the preceding step function configuration because this is related to the infrastructure deployment. Here, you need to configure the infrastructure-related stuff associated with this **StateMachine**.

You might have also noticed <<Lambda Role>> and <<StepFunction Role>> defined for **RoleArn** under Properties. To create these roles, you have to log in to the AWS Console and then go to the IAM service. Under the IAM service, create a Lambda role by attaching **AWSLambdaFullAccess** and **AmazonS3FullAccess** policies. To create a step function role, attach **CloudWatchFullAccess** and **AWSLambdaRole** policies.

EventBridge

As discussed in *Chapter 6, Communication Patterns and Service Discovery*, messaging patterns help us develop loosely coupled applications. AWS introduces EventBridge, which is a serverless, highly available, and scalable event bus that connects applications. This makes it easy to build event-driven applications and based on rules, you can route your events to different AWS services. To configure EventBridge, we first need to create an event bus.

The following screenshot depicts two event buses, default and **OrderProcessorBus**. The default event bus, as the name suggests, is the default event bus for your account. You can use it to subscribe to events. However, I have created **OrderProcessorBus** for this tutorial and will show you the steps of its creation:

Figure 7.4: *Event Bridge Event bus*

Create event bus

Creating an event bus in EventBridge is quite simple. The following screenshot shows the naming of the event bus. However, if you grant permission to a different AWS account or organization to access your event bus, then other options need to be considered. By default, those are unchecked.

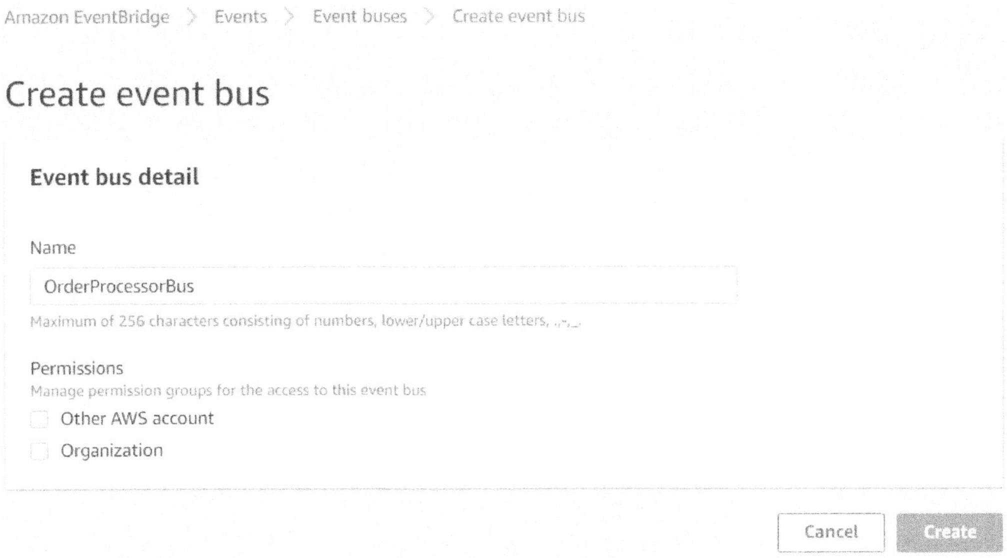

Amazon EventBridge > Events > Event buses > Create event bus

Create event bus

Event bus detail

Name

OrderProcessorBus

Maximum of 256 characters consisting of numbers, lower/upper case letters, .,-,_.

Permissions
Manage permission groups for the access to this event bus

☐ Other AWS account

☐ Organization

Cancel   **Create**

Figure 7.5: *Create Event Bus*

Create Rule

Rules are an important part of EventBridge. Rules are tied to the event bus and are configured to route the events to one or more targets (usually AWS services). You can pass the event to target as it is or can modify it if needed.

For the **OrderProcessorBus,** we have created a rule and named it order-catchall.

Name and description

Name

order-catchall

Maximum of 64 characters consisting of lower/upper case letters, ., -, _.

Description - *optional*

Enter description

Figure 7.6: *Event bus name and description*

Configure patterns

Now, the following screenshot shows the configure patterns. The event pattern makes this a rule that is triggered when an event matching the pattern occurs. You can either use a pre-defined pattern by service or create your custom patterns.

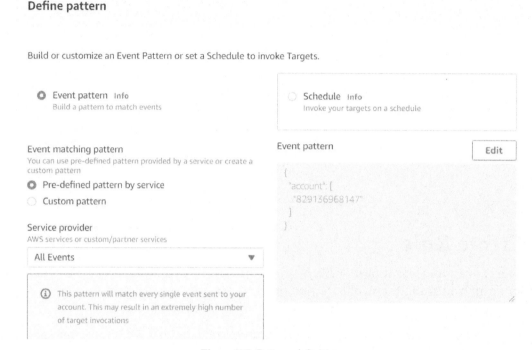

Figure 7.7: Pattern definition

Now we have to configure targets. Targets are the AWS services that are invoked when an event occurs in the **OrderProcessorBus** event bus. As of now, its limit is 5 targets per rule.

Configure targets

EventBridge target is a resource that is being called when a rule is triggered.

The following screenshot shows the configuration of two target groups. One for step function and another for CloudWatch. CloudWatch target is useful when you want to log your incoming events for debugging or analytics:

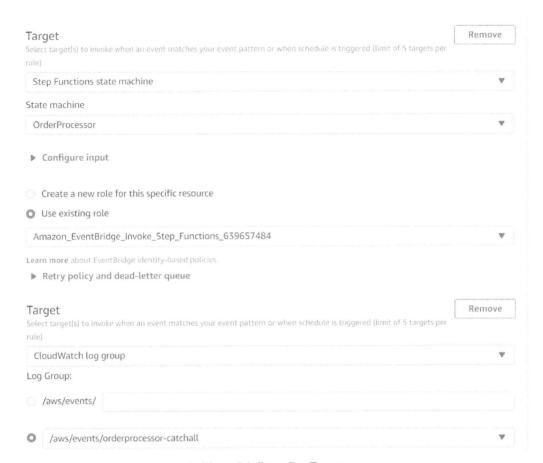

Figure 7.8: *Event Bus Targets*

Connecting microservices

Now that we have discussed the different services of our application and how to configure it, it's time to connect these services to achieve some business functionality.

The following diagram shows the **OrderProcessor** step function performing tasks, like processing orders, processing payments, and sending an email. We want to access this functionality from outside as an endpoint through the API gateway so that client applications can post request messages. However, we want the endpoint to be asynchronous and reactive so that the client doesn't have to wait for the response before further processing. So, we have introduced an EventBridge and created OrderProcessorBus to route events to the configured AWS service targets.

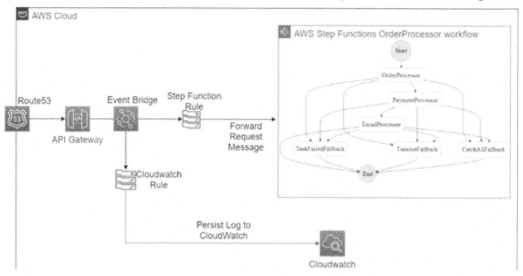

Figure 7.9: Overall architecture

Configuring API gateway

As we already know that API gateway is an API management tool that acts as a reverse proxy between the client and the backend service. In this example, we will create API resources/methods and map them to the EventBridge. In doing so, incoming requests to the API gateway will get redirect to the EventBridge and from there they will be routed to the specific AWS resources. API gateway doesn't know about the services which we will use. It is only responsible for forwarding the request to the EventBridge, making it loosely coupled.

Create resource

The basic entity of the REST architecture is resources. To access resources, we need to design **Uniform Resource Identifiers (URI)**, which allow a client to access the server content using a predefined format and methods, like POST, GET, PUT, etc.

The following screenshot shows the creation of a **processOrder** resource:

New Child Resource

Use this page to create a new child resource for your resource. ⊛

Configure as proxy resource   ☐ **❶**

Resource Name*   processorder

Resource Path*   / processorder

You can add path parameters using brackets. For example, the resource path **{username}** represents a path parameter called 'username'. Configuring /{proxy+} as a proxy resource catches all requests to its sub-resources. For example, it works for a GET request to /foo. To handle requests to /, add a new ANY method on the / resource.

Enable API Gateway CORS   ☐ **❶**

* Required   Cancel   **Create Resource**

Figure 7.10: Add New Resource

Note: You can also select the Enable API Gateway CORS option. In that case, a new OPTIONS method will get created automatically and you will have to configure it the same way as step 2 mentioned further in this chapter.

Create method

Now, create a POST method. For integration, type select **AWS Service** since we want the API gateway to forward the request to the EventBridge bus. Select CloudWatch events in the AWS service section. Use ANY for the HTTP method. For actions, use **PutEvents,** which is an EventBridge event to publish into the event bus. Create a new EventBridge- role by attaching **CloudWatchFullAccess** and **AmazonEventBridgeFullAccess** policies.

Also, edit the Trust relationship with the following JSON to provide permission to the API gateway to publish in EventBridge bus:

```
1.   {
2.     "Version": "2012-10-17",
3.     "Statement": [
4.       {
5.         "Sid": "",
6.         "Effect": "Allow",
7.         "Principal": {
8.           "Service": [
9.             "apigateway.amazonaws.com",
10.            "events.amazonaws.com"
11.          ]
```

```
12.            },
13.            "Action": "sts:AssumeRole"
14.         }
15.      ]
16.  }
```

Figure 7.11: Add New Method

Configure headers

The HTTP headers are used to pass additional information between the client and the server with a request or response. Before forwarding the request from the API gateway to the EventBridge, we have to add additional headers for the EventBridge to process the request properly.

The following screenshot shows the values in the HTTP Headers section. This is a critical configuration for the EventBridge to process and forward the request:

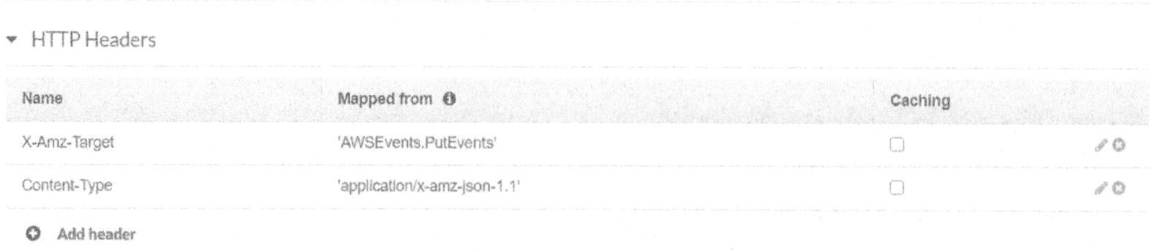

Figure 7.12: Add Event Bridge Customized Headers

Configure mapping template

Next, we have an additional configuration in the mapping templates. A mapping template is useful to map the incoming requests to the outgoing custom messages. The following screenshot shows the API gateway executing the mapping when the content-type is of **application/json:**

JSON in the mapping template starts with the #set. Entries are a collection of entry which define an event in your system and are of the type **PutEventsRequestEntry.** **PutEventsRequestEntry** type contains **DetailType**, **EventBusName**, **Resources**, **Source**, **Time** and **Detail**. Here, I have entered **DetailType** as "**json**" and **EventBusName** as "**OrderProcessorBus**" (that we created in the preceding section), source as "**Order**" and map **Detail** property to the payload of the upcoming message.

Figure 7.13: Mapping Template

> Note: Give proper DetailType in the Entries collection. It is a free-form string that is used to decide what fields are expected in the Detail section.

Add method response

Now add HTTP status in the method response. It is important to add an HTTP response here because we will directly post the message to EventBridge. Once the message gets posted in the EventBridge, we need to intimate the client with a 200 status code that the request is successfully processed. The API gateway will map the 200 status code in the response defined in the method response.

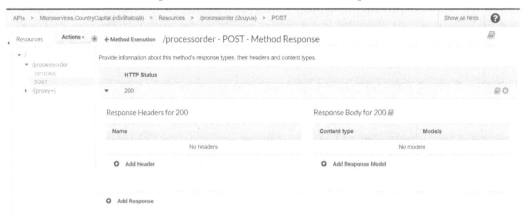

Figure 7.14: Add Method Response

Deploy and test

Finally, deploy the changes by creating a new stage production as shown in the following screenshot:

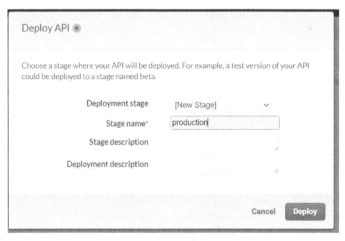

Figure 7.15: Deploy API

It's time to test if everything is configured properly. Once deployed, open the POST method, copy the URL, and suffix "**/processorder**" to the URL in the POST method URL of the postman. If it is successful, you will get **EventId** as a response, as shown in the following figure:

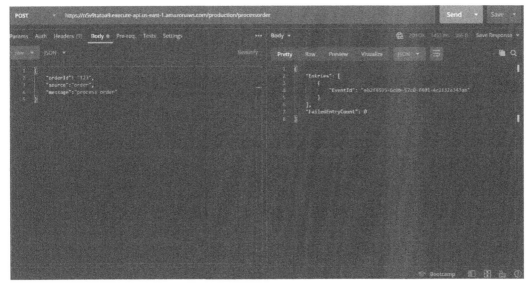

Figure 7.16: Test API using PostMan

EventBridge drastically changes the way AWS services can communicate with events. It is quite powerful and you can integrate with almost all the necessary AWS services with it. You will find the code in my GitHub repository,

https://github.com/sarkarstanmoy/AWS-Microservices/tree/master/Chapter7/ StepFunctions/OrderProcessor, for reference.

Conclusion

In this chapter, we saw how to create **/configure** the step function and EventBridge. We also configured the API gateway to publish events on the event bus. Since EventBridge is gaining popularity, it will be useful if you keep this tool in your toolbox while making decisions for event-driven architecture. In the next chapter, we will look at another important aspect of event-driven architecture, i.e., monitoring. Monitoring your microservices in an event-driven architecture is a challenge and we will use some of the services provided by AWS to overcome this.

Points to remember

- **EventBridge** was formerly called Amazon CloudWatch Events.

- AWS step function is used to orchestrate serverless functions into business-critical operations.

- States are the individual building blocks of step function which contain business logic to perform.

- To coordinate between the states, we need a state machine where we can design our flow of execution.

- State machines are built using Amazon States Language, which is JSON-structured to represent the elements.

- EventBridge is a serverless, highly available, and scalable event bus that connects applications.

- Rules are tied to the event bus and are configured to route the events to one or more targets.

- The event pattern makes this a rule that is triggered when an event matching the pattern occurs.

Multiple choice questions

1. **What was EventBridge formerly called?**
   a) Amazon CloudWatch Events
   b) Events
   c) Amazon event bus

2. **EventBridge rules are used to route events to one or more ---?**
   a) Event bus
   b) Targets
   c) Rules

3. **Rules are tied to ____?**
   a) Targets
   b) Event bus
   c) None of the above

4. **Step function state machines are built using____?**
   a) YAML
   b) Amazon State Language
   c) None of the above

Answer

1. a
2. b
3. b
4. b

CHAPTER 8

Distributed Monitoring

Everything fails, all the time.

--- Werner Vogels

Introduction

Microservices are parts of the system which can be independently deployed, are language-agnostics, and resilient. Resiliency is achieved in microservice because of the distributed nature where one part of the system failure might not tear down the whole system. This resiliency helps the developers to identify the issue and fix it independently. However, for developers to figure out the exact issue is one of the challenges in a distributed system. So, monitoring tools are necessary for a distributed system for ideal debugging. In this chapter, we will discuss some of the services provided by AWS, like CloudWatch and X-Ray to monitor, log, and trace. Since microservice communicates with each other, these monitoring tools play a major role in identifying and resolving the issues in event-driven distributed systems.

Structure

- CloudWatch
  - o   Monitoring

      o   Logging
- X-ray
  - o   X-Ray graph
  - o   X-Ray tracing

Objective

In this chapter, you will learn how to monitor microservice using AWS CloudWatch and X-Ray services. You will also learn about the different graphs generated by these services and how to use trace to resolve issues.

By the end of this chapter, you will get efficient enough to analyze CloudWatch logs and X-Ray traces.

CloudWatch

Amazon CloudWatch is a centralized monitoring and logging service for most AWS services. It is used to store logs in log groups, raise events, and analyze logs for troubleshooting. Since this book is mainly based on developing a serverless application, we will discuss how to monitor Lambda functions using CloudWatch.

Monitoring

If your serverless application fails in production and proper monitoring tools have not been configured to raise alarms, it might lead to the entire application failure. The good news is AWS Lambda does automatically track the number of requests, number of invocations, and errors. It also publishes CloudWatch metrics which can be used to raise CloudWatch events for real-time notification.

There are a few important metrics that Lambda captures automatically on behalf of our application that we will discuss here concerning our **CountryCapitalServerlessApi** deployed in the previous chapter:

- Invocations

  It is the number of times Lambda is invoked during a time interval. By default, it shows a 5 minutes period for a span of 1 hour. You can change the period to view historic data.

  The following screenshot shows 14 invocations on the 9th of September (number of times Lambda function invoked during a time) :

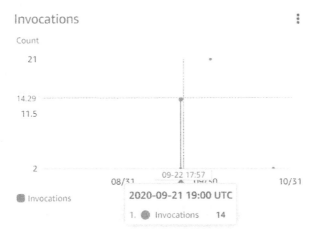

Figure 8.1: *Number of Lambda Invocations*

- Duration

  This metrics is used to understand how your Lambda function performs during a period. It shows the maximum, average, and minimum duration of the Lambda function. If the maximum or average is too high, it might indicate you need to optimize your Lambda function. You can also add CloudWatch events based on these metrics to report slow-performing Lambda in case it crosses the threshold limit of maximum or average duration.

  The following screenshot shows the metrics of **CountryCapitalServerlessApi** where the average execution time to complete the process is about 758 msec:

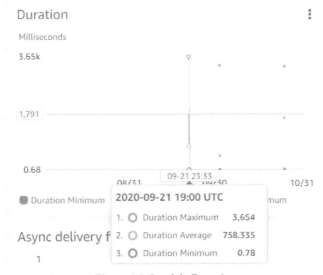

Figure 8.2: *Lambda Duration*

- Error count and success rate

    This metric is used to show the number of times Lambda execution fails and the percentage of success. This metric is used to understand the success rate of your Lambda function. If the number of error count is more than the success rate, it needs to investigate the root cause.

    The following screenshot shows that no error occurs with a success rate of 100%:

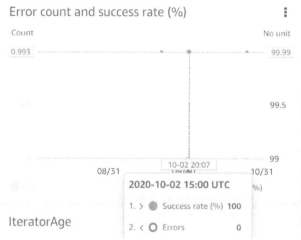

Figure 8.3: Lambda Error Count and Success rate

- Throttles

    AWS Lambda, when invoked for the first time, creates an instance of the function and starts processing. After it finishes the process, it will wait for subsequent requests. However, while processing the request, if more requests come up, then an additional instance of Lambda will get created so that the concurrent Lambda function can be invoked. But it has a limitation based on the region. As per the current AWS burst, concurrency quotas are as follows:

    o   3000 – US West (Oregon), US East (N. Virginia), Europe (Ireland)

    o   1000 – Asia Pacific (Tokyo), Europe (Frankfurt), US East (Ohio)

    o   500 – Other Regions

    Above this limit, the Lambda functions will begin to throttle (literal meaning is to get choked or strangled) and the execution will fail. This metric is used to monitor the number of Lambda function execution fail due to throttling.

    The following screenshot shows 0 throttling. This means that Lambda's execution has not exceeded the concurrency quota limit of the region. However, in high load, this number can vary. In case of a high load, if your Lambda function starts throttling, it means you need to dissect the reason behind the long execution time.

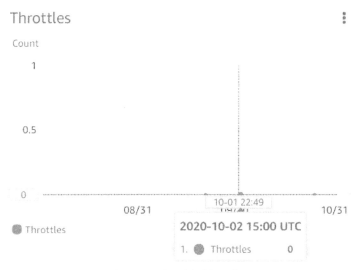

Figure 8.4: *Lambda Throttles*

- Concurrent executions

  AWS Lambda scales up and down as per the load. If the number of requests is high, the Lambda function scales up and multiple Lambda instances start simultaneously. The number of Lambda instances run parallel denotes the number of concurrent executions. Going above the concurrency limit of a region, your Lambda function begins to throttle.

  In the following screenshot, only 2 instances of Lambda functions are executed concurrently to process the incoming requests.

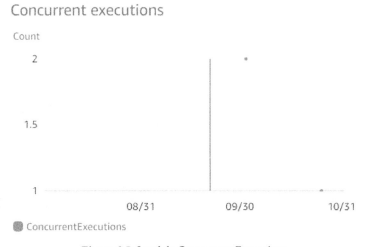

Figure 8.5: *Lambda Concurrent Executions*

- Async delivery failures

  This is used to monitor the number of times Lambda fails to store messages in dead-letter queues or delivers a message to the destination asynchronously.

  Usually, messages are stored in a dead-letter queue when Lambda is not able to process messages. As per the following screenshot, there are not any async delivery failures for our **CountryCapital serverless** API.

Figure 8.6: Lambda Async Delivery Failures

Note: To see the monitoring metrics, you have to go to the Lambda function and click on the monitoring tab.

Logging

Lambda logs are stored in CloudWatch under the log groups. Each log groups have log streams that were created based on timestamp. You can use these logs for further analysis by funneling them into AWS log insights analysis tools.

The following screenshot shows the log group of **CountryCapitalServerless** API. As you have noted, the log group created for Lambda has a suffix of **/AWS/lambda**. Inside the log group, you will have multiple log streams. There is also an option *"Retention"* in the log group to specify the number of days you want to retain your logs. You can create a subscription filter to raise events for any specific log message, for example, in case of a 500 error, you can notify the developers through email:

Figure 8.7: CloudWatch Logs

X-Ray

AWS X-Ray is another service to monitor the distributed systems. Using an X-Ray, you can trace your request and understand its flow. If any error occurs during the flow, an X-Ray will show it as a graph. You can also create an X-Ray group to segregate traces concerning environments.

You can enable X-Ray either from the AWS console or through the CloudFormation template. Here, I will show you how to enable from the AWS console.

- Lambda

Once you enable X-Ray in Lambda, it starts to run X-Ray daemon which intercepts requests and records a segment with invocation details. X-Ray daemon is a software application that listens to the traffic on UDP 2000 and forwards the gathered information to AWS X-Ray API. X-Ray segment is a JSON document of the maximum size of 64 kb to record information of request, application details, and subsegment. Subsegment is the metadata of segments.

The following screenshot shows the navigation to Lambda monitoring tools to enable X-Ray in Lambda function:

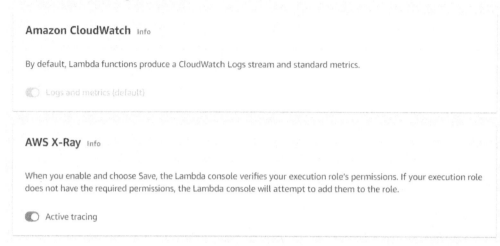

Figure 8.8: Enable X-Ray in Lambda

-

- Step function

  To enable step function to write X-Ray trace, make sure to give X-Ray policies access to step function role. I have added **XRayFullAccess** policies to the "*StepFunctionRole*" role.

  The following screenshot shows how to enable the X-Ray in a step function. You first log in to the AWS console, then go to a step function, and then click on Edit. Scroll down to enable X-Ray tracing:

Figure 8.9: Enable X-Ray in Step Function

- API gateway

  Enabling X-Ray in the API gateway helps you analyze the request for underlying services in an X-Ray graph or tracing.

The following screenshot shows how to enable X-Ray in an API gateway. First, go to Stages. Then, under the stage, go to the Log/Tracing section to enable X-Ray tracing.

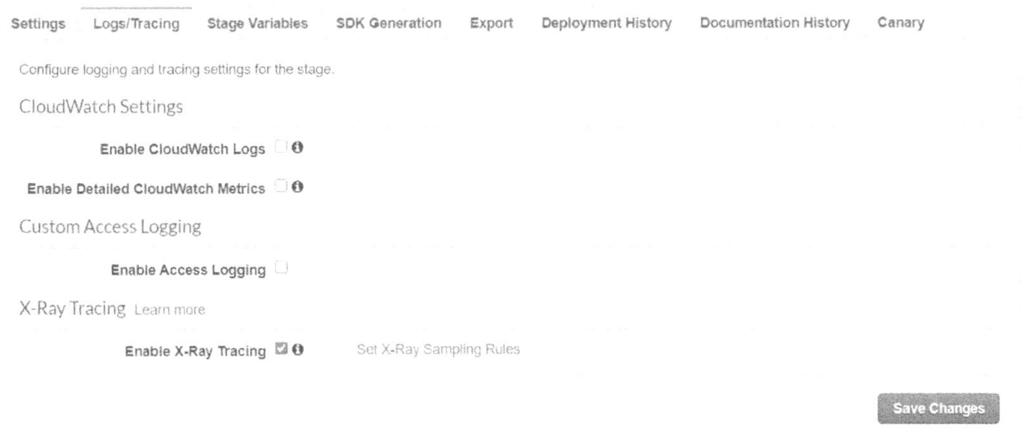

Settings   Logs/Tracing   Stage Variables   SDK Generation   Export   Deployment History   Documentation History   Canary

Configure logging and tracing settings for the stage.

CloudWatch Settings

Enable CloudWatch Logs ☐ ❶

Enable Detailed CloudWatch Metrics ☐ ❶

Custom Access Logging

Enable Access Logging ☐

X-Ray Tracing Learn more

Enable X-Ray Tracing ☑ ❶   Set X-Ray Sampling Rules

Save Changes

Figure 8.10: *Enable X-Ray in API Gateway*

X-Ray graph

Once you enable X-Ray for all the services mentioned in the previous section, you get to visualize the diagram of data flow, as shown in the following figure:

Figure 8.11: *X-Ray Dependency Graph*

X-Ray tracing

For further analysis of data, the flow goes to traces and selects the trace. Under the timeline, you will find different metrics related to the data flow, as shown in the following figure:

Figure 8.12: X-Ray Tracing

Conclusion

In this chapter, we came through a few of the AWS services which help in monitoring the distributed systems. However, this is only an overview and if interested, you can go much deeper into these services, customize as per your need, and create CloudWatch events for alerts. In the next chapter, we will see some of the security aspects of the distributed systems and how to protect your APIs from anonymous access.

Points to remember

- Amazon CloudWatch is a centralized monitoring and logging service for most AWS services.

- AWS Lambda throttling happens when the concurrent execution exceeds the concurrency quotas.

- Lambda stores failed messages to the dead-letter queue.

- Lambda logs are stored in CloudWatch under the log groups.

- Each CloudWatch log group has timestamped log streams.

- AWS X-Ray is another service to monitor a distributed system.

- X-Ray metrics can be analyzed through dependency graphs or tracing.

Multiple choice questions

1. **What do CloudWatch log groups contain?**

   a) Events

   b) Log streams

   c) Log events

2. **What AWS services are used to log and monitor the distributed systems?**

   a) CloudWatch

   b) X-Ray

   c) A B

2. Lambda stores failed messages to ____?

   a) Queues

   b) Event bus

   c) Dead-letter queue

Answer

1. b

2. c

3. c

CHAPTER 9
Security

> **Security is not a product but a process.**
>
> --- *Bruce Schneier (Founder and CTO, Counterpane Internet Security, Inc)*

Introduction

In every application, security plays a major role to protect your application from malicious attacks. However, developers don't want to spend too much time integrating the security layer in their application and look for a solution that is reliable, efficient, and customizable. To make it easier for developers, AWS has provided the Cognito service for authentication and authorization. Lambda authorizer is another authorization technique used explicitly for API gateway to implement a custom authorization scheme that uses the bearer token authentication. In this chapter, we will discuss how to configure the Cognito service and Lambda authorizer with an example to integrate with the API gateway.

Structure

Security strategies

- Lambda authorizer

- AWS Cognito

o JWT token

o Request flow design

o Cognito configuration

o Integrate with API gateway

Objective

In this chapter, you will learn the basic usage of the JWT token, how to integrate Lambda authorizer with the API gateway and configure Cognito service to authenticate and authorize incoming requests.

At the end of this chapter, you will have enough understanding of the security services provided by AWS for authentication and authorization.

Security strategies

Here we will discuss different AWS security strategies concerning AWS API gateway to secure your endpoints. For the demo, we will add security to our **processOrder** endpoint using Lambda authorizer and Cognito service.

Lambda authorizer

Lambda authorizer is an API gateway feature to authorizer API using the Lambda function. It is useful for a custom authorization scheme.

There are two types of Lambda authorizers:

- **Token-based**: Token such as **JSON Web Token** (**JWT**) or OAuth token is used to authenticate the caller identity.

- **Request-based**: Validate the caller's identity by using a combination of headers, query string parameters, stage variables, and context variables.

Few advantages of Lambda authorizer are centralized codebases to maintain the authorization for API methods and caching responses. The disadvantage with Lambda authorizer is that the developers need to add an authorization header for every API method irrespective of their access level.

The following diagram shows the steps involved while validating the authorization token. Route 53 forwards the request to the API gateway which will pass it to the Lambda authorizer for authorization. Lambda authorizer will respond with either Allow or Deny IAM policy. The policy will be validated by the IAM policy manager and based on the authorization response, it will either authorize or unauthorize the request:

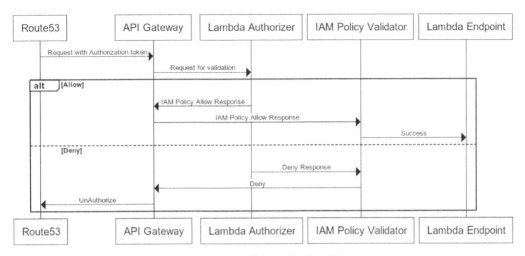

Figure 9.1: *Lambda Authorizer Flow*

The following screenshot shows the addition of Lambda authorization on API gateway for our existing **OrderProcessor** endpoint, which will intercept requests to validate the token value:

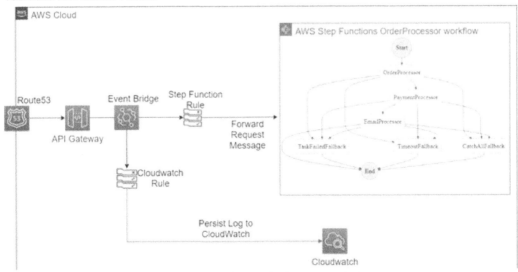

Figure 9.2: *Lambda Authorizer system design*

Steps to follow to integrate Lambda authorizer with API gateway:

1. Create a Lambda function for custom authorization. For this demo, we will create a Lambda function that will generate an Allow policy if the token value is allowed, and a Deny policy by default.

   The following code shows the extraction of the authorization value from the input request header. Based on its value (Allow or Deny), we will generate an IAM policy. GeneratePolicy method generates the standard IAM policy document by accepting the principalId, which is a unique id, effect, which is either Allow or Deny and resource, which is the MethodArn of the incoming request. The generated document is then passed to the IAM policy validator to validate and execute the policy:

```
1.   namespace TokenAuthorizer
2.   {
3.       public class Functions
4.       {
5.           [LambdaSerializer(typeof(Amazon.Lambda.Serialization.
             Json.JsonSerializer))]
6.                       public  APIGatewayCustomAuthorizerResponse
             FunctionHandler(APIGatewayCustomAuthorizerRequest    input,
             ILambdaContext context)
7.             {
8.                 var token = input.AuthorizationToken;
9.                 switch (token)
10.                {
11.                    case "allow":
12.                        return GeneratePolicy("user", "Allow",
             input.MethodArn);
13.                    default:
14.                        return GeneratePolicy("user", "Deny",
             input.MethodArn);
15.
16.                }
17.            }
18.
19.                 private  APIGatewayCustomAuthorizerResponse
             GeneratePolicy(string  principalId,  string  effect,  string
             resource)
20.            {
21.
22.                APIGatewayCustomAuthorizerResponse authResponse
             = new APIGatewayCustomAuthorizerResponse();
23.                        authResponse.PolicyDocument   =   new
             APIGatewayCustomAuthorizerPolicy();
```

```
24.                 authResponse.PolicyDocument.Version = "2012-10-
        17";
25.             authResponse.PolicyDocument.Statement = new System.
        Collections.Generic.List<APIGatewayCustomAuthorizerPolicy.
        IAMPolicyStatement>();
26.                 System.Collections.Generic.HashSet<string>
        Actions = new System.Collections.Generic.HashSet<string>();
27.             Actions.Add("execute-api:Invoke");
28.           System.Collections.Generic.HashSet<string> Resources
        = new System.Collections.Generic.HashSet<string>();
29.             Resources.Add(resource);
30.
31.             authResponse.PolicyDocument.Statement.Add(new
        APIGatewayCustomAuthorizerPolicy.IAMPolicyStatement()
32.             {
33.                 Action = Actions,
34.                 Effect = effect,
35.                 Resource = Resources
36.             });
37.
38.
39.             return authResponse;
40.         }
41.
42.     }
43. }
```

2. After the TokenAuthorizer Lambda gets deployed, open AWS Console and navigate to the API gateway. Under Microservices.CountryCapital API (created in the previous demo), go to authorizers. Create an authorizer by selecting the Lambda authorizer function. The token source will denote

which request header value to use for authorization. Enable caching by the default 5 minutes, as shown in the following screenshot:

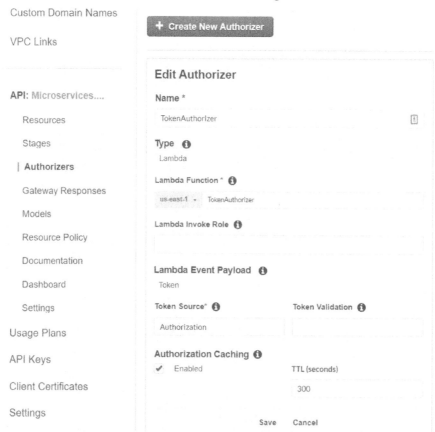

Figure 9.3: *Create API Gateway Lambda Authorizer*

3. Now, go to **Resouces** -> **/processorder Resouce** -> **POST** method. Under Method Request, select Authorization as Token Authorizer created in the previous steps, As shown in the following screenshot:

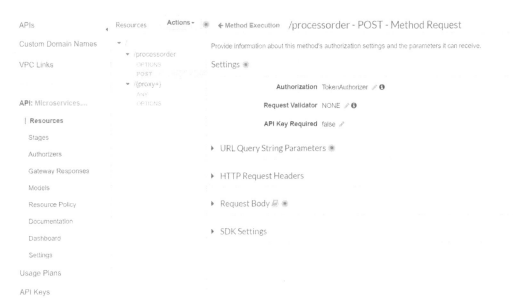

Figure 9.4: Assign Token Authorizer to API gateway

4. Use postman to validate your settings

The following screenshot shows the success message when we pass Allow in the authorization header:

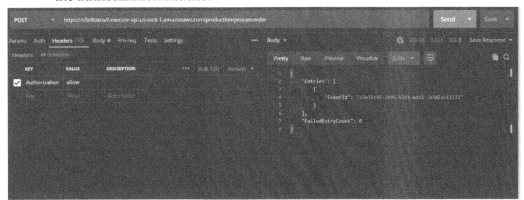

Figure 9.5: Postman Screenshot Success

The following screenshot shows the unauthorized access when we pass Deny in the authorization header:

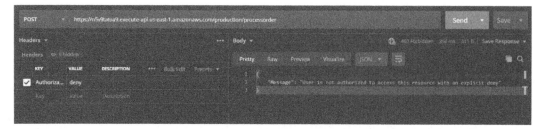

Figure 9.6: Postman Screenshot Unauthorize

AWS Cognito

AWS Cognito is a centralized, AWS-managed service for user management that enables users to sign in through mobile and web. To manage users in AWS Cognito, create a user pool and assign it to your application. Cognito will authenticate the users on your behalf and pass the token to the request header for authorization. Since Cognito is itself such a large service, we will not discuss it in detail as it is out of scope for this book. This chapter mainly concentrates on how to secure authenticate Lambda endpoint using Cognito. We will discuss the basic setup and integrate it with the API gateway.

JWT token

In this chapter, we will use the JWT token-based authentication. JWT is a modern approach to pass information for authorization as a JSON object. JWT consists of three parts:

- **Header**: Used to identify the signing algorithm
- **Payload**: Contains users claim and data
- **Signature**: Base 64 encoding of header and payload

Request flow design

The following diagram shows the steps involved while validating the authorization token using Cognito. Route 53 forwards the request to the API gateway, which will pass it to the Cognito authorizer for authorization. The Cognito authorizer will validate the token and respond with either Allow or Deny. The response will be validated based on the authorization response that will either authorize or unauthorize the request:

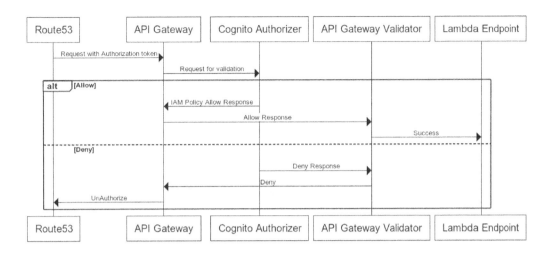

Figure 9.7: *Cognito Authorizer Flow*

The following diagram shows the architectural design of the processOrder with the Cognito authorizer involved. The request message that comes to the API gateway will get validated by Cognito using the authorization token and based on the result, it will either allow or reject the request:

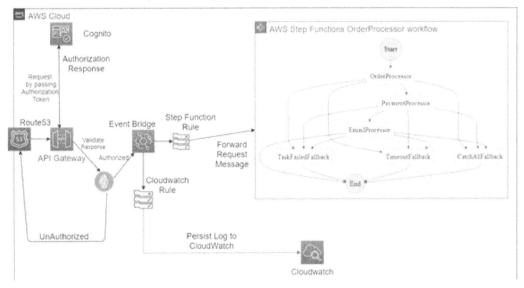

Figure 9.8: *Cognito Authorizer System Design*

Cognito configuration

To start configuring Cognito, we will start with creating a user pool. User pool is a user directory that will authenticate the user and once authenticated, it will provide JWT tokens.

The following diagram shows the creation of a user pool **processorder-user** pool and the selection of default settings. For our demo, user pool default settings are more than sufficient:

Figure 9.9: Create Cognito User Pool

Now, after the pool is created, you can see the default settings are set on your behalf.

The following diagram shows the settings, like minimum password length should be 8, pool id, pool ARN, and so on:

User Pools | Federated Identities

processorder-userpool

General settings	
Users and groups	Pool Id ▓▓▓▓▓▓▓▓▓▓
Attributes	Pool ARN am:aws:cognito-idp:us-east-1:829136968147:userpool/us-east-1_GKvnPcxax
Policies	
MFA and verifications	
Advanced security	Estimated number of users 1
Message customizations	
Tags	Required attributes email
Devices	Alias attributes none
App clients	Username attributes none
Triggers	Enable case insensitivity? Yes
Analytics	Custom attributes Choose custom attributes...
App integration	
App client settings	
Domain name	Minimum password length 8
UI customization	Password policy uppercase letters, lowercase letters, special characters, numbers
Resource servers	User sign ups allowed? Users can sign themselves up
Federation	
Identity providers	
Attribute mapping	FROM email address Default
	Email Delivery through Amazon SES No

Figure 9.10: Cognito User Pool Details

User pools are associated with the app clients to authenticate users. The app clients are responsible for user authentication. Usually, separate app clients are created if your application runs on the web and mobile respectively. The app clients do have different authentication mechanisms and you can configure which authentication flow you want for your application. Types of auth flow configurations are as follows:

1. **ALLOW_ADMIN_USER_PASSWORD_AUTH**: This is used for server-to-server authentication.

2. **ALLOW_CUSTOM_AUTH**: This is used to implement your own customized authentication rules. For this Cognito, provide a Lambda function trigger where you can map your Lambda function and it will get triggered during the authentication process.

3. **ALLOW_USER_PASSWORD_AUTH**: This is used for client-side authentication that uses a username and password.

4. **ALLOW_USER_SRP_AUTH**: This is like **ALLOW_USER_PASSWORD_AUTH** except it uses the **Secure Remote Password** (**SRP**). SRP is a cryptographic authentication for password-based authentication over an insecure channel. SRP diminishes man-in-the-middle attack.

5. **ALLOW_REFRESH_TOKEN_AUTH**: Refresh token is used to retrieve a new token when an existing token expired. The user does not have to log in every time to get a new token.

The following screenshot shows the selection of **ALLOW_ADMIN_USER_PASSWORD_ AUTH**, **ALLOW_USER_SRP_AUTH**, and **ALLOW_REFRESH_TOKEN_AUTH** auth flow configurations:

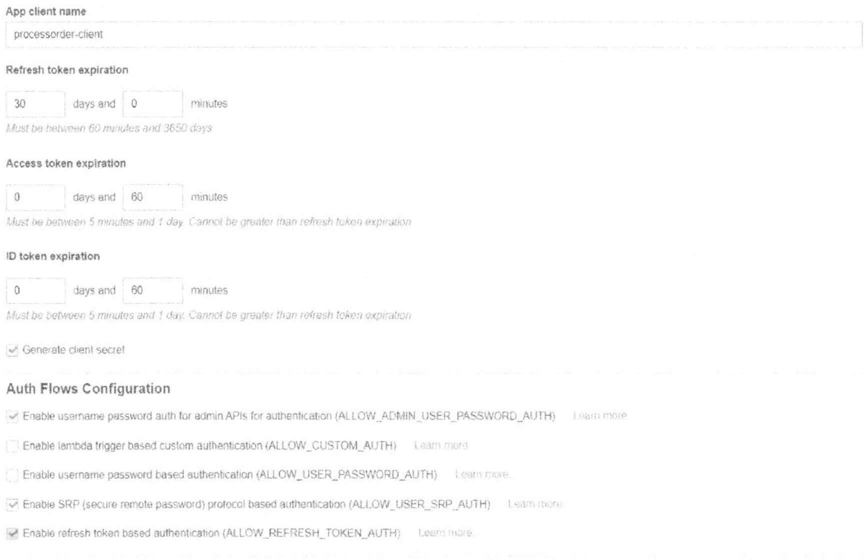

Figure 9.11: Create Cognito App Client

Once the app client is created, you will get the app client id and app client secret. These two values are used to authenticate users from your application.

The following diagram shows the masked app client and client secret of processorder-client which we created to authenticate processorder API:

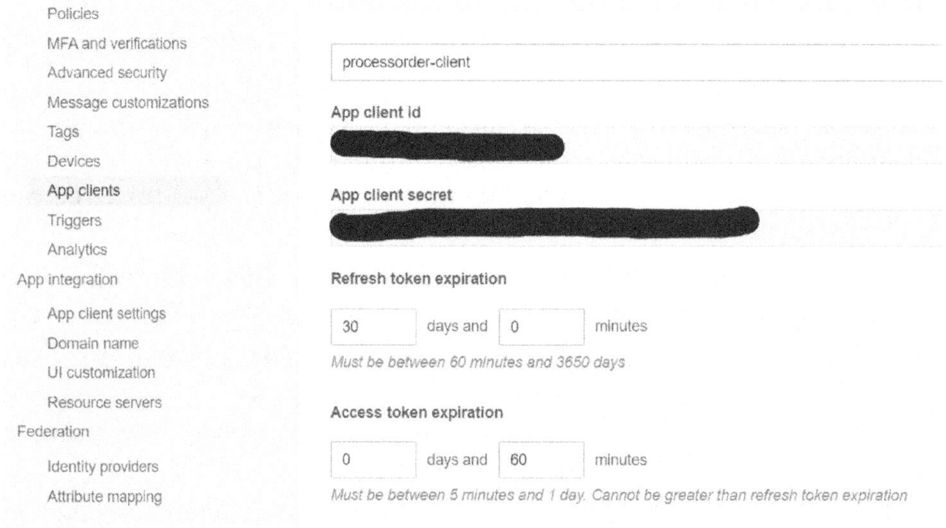

Figure 9.12: Cognito App Client Details

Next, we must create a sample to test our configuration. The following diagram shows the creation of an **aws_hero** username and temporary password:

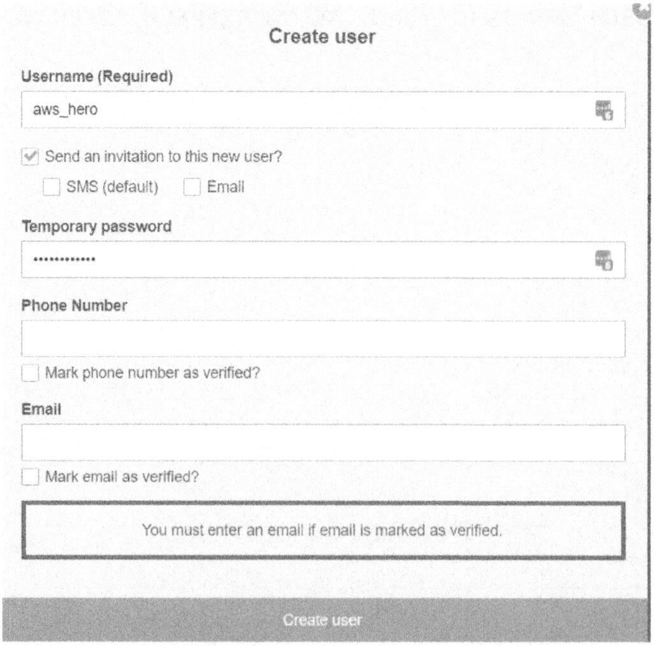

Figure 9.13: Create Cognito User

Once the user is created, the account status will become **FORCE_CHANGE_PASSWORD**. To confirm it, we need to run the following command explicitly:

```
aws    cognito-idp    admin-set-user-password    --user-pool-id    <<poolid>>
--username <<username>> --password <<password>> --permanent
```

In an ideal scenario, you will get the email provided in the preceding configuration for password confirmation:

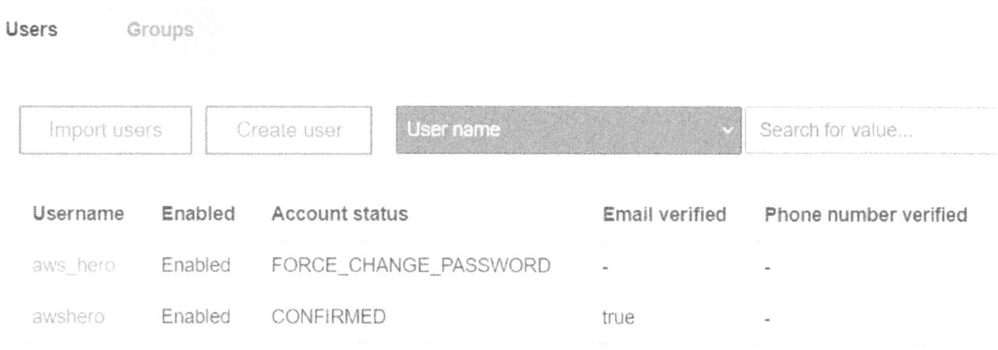

Username	Enabled	Account status		Email verified	Phone number verified
aws_hero	Enabled	FORCE_CHANGE_PASSWORD		-	-
awshero	Enabled	CONFIRMED		true	-

Figure 9.14: *New created user account status*

Finally, we run the following sample code to generate an access token and pass it on to the authorization header of the application request. To retrieve a token from the Cognito service a new AuthRequest is initialized by using **ClientId**, **UserPoolId**, and **ADMIN_USER_PASSWORD_AUTH**. Pass the username, password, and secret hash (which we generated using the custom code) as AuthParameters and get the access token as a response. This access token is then used to pass along the request to the API gateway to validate the request:

```
1.    class Program
2.        {
3.            static void Main(string[] args)
4.            {
5.                string CLIENT_ID = "<<ClientId>>";
6.                string USERPOOL_ID = "<<PoolId>>";
7.                string USERNAME = "<<UserName>>";
8.                string PASSWORD = "<<Password>> ";
9.                string SECRET = "<<Secret>>";
10.
11.                    AmazonCognitoIdentityProviderClient provider =
      new    AmazonCognitoIdentityProviderClient(FallbackRegionFactory.
      GetRegionEndpoint());
12.
```

```
13.                 var request = new AdminInitiateAuthRequest()
14.                 {
15.                     AuthFlow = AuthFlowType.ADMIN_USER_PASSWORD_AUTH,
16.                     ClientId= CLIENT_ID,
17.                     UserPoolId= USERPOOL_ID,
18.
19.                 };
20.
21.                 request.AuthParameters.Add("USERNAME", USERNAME);
22.                 request.AuthParameters.Add("PASSWORD", PASSWORD);
23.                         request.AuthParameters.Add("SECRET_HASH",
        GenerateSecretHash(USERNAME, CLIENT_ID, SECRET));
24.             var response = provider.AdminInitiateAuthAsync(request).
        Result;
25.                     Console.WriteLine(response.AuthenticationResult.
        AccessToken);
26.                 Console.ReadLine();
27.
28.         }
29.
30.           public static string GenerateSecretHash(string userName,
        string appClientId, string appSecretKey)
31.           {
32.                 var str = $"{userName}{appClientId}";
33.
34.                 var userData = Encoding.UTF8.GetBytes(str);
35.                 var secretKey = Encoding.UTF8.GetBytes(appSecretKey);
36.
37.                     return Convert.ToBase64String(HmacSHA256(userData,
        secretKey));
38.           }
39.
40.         public static byte[] HmacSHA256(byte[] data, byte[] key)
41.           {
42.                 using (var shaAlgorithm = new HMACSHA256(key))
```

```
43.                    {
44.                        var result = shaAlgorithm.ComputeHash(data);
45.                        return result;
46.                    }
47.                }
48.
49.
50.        }
```

Integrate with API gateway

To integrate Cognito with the API gateway, we need to first create an authorizer. The type of the authorizer must be Cognito and we need to select the user pool created in the previous steps. Also, we need to mention the token source which is the request header. The following screenshot shows the configuration used for this demo:

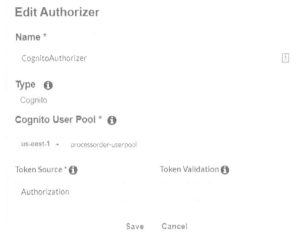

Figure 9.15: Add Authorizer for Cognito in API Gateway

Finally, we need to map the Cognito authorizer for the authorization of the API gateway. Make sure to add OAuth scope, which is **aws.cognito.signin.user. admin**. In the real-time application, you can provide a custom scope for your application while configuring the app settings. The scope will be helpful for authorization and will decide the APIs your request can access.

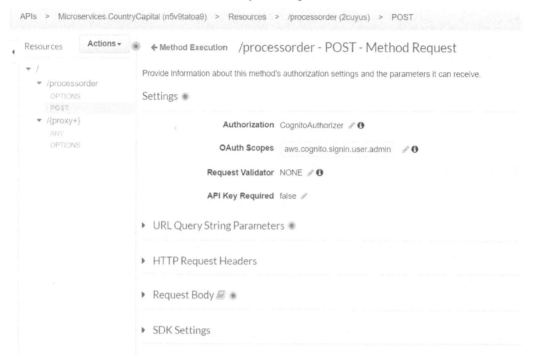

Figure 9.16: Assign Cognito Authorizer to API Gateway

Conclusion

In this chapter, we discussed two types of API gateway authorization that can be used to secure your API gateway endpoint. Lambda authorizer is for custom authorization to control access to your API which uses a custom authorization token-based authentication strategy. However, Cognito is a fully managed service used for an enterprise-level application. Cognito allows the users to sign in using social identity providers as well as enterprise providers, such as Microsoft Active directory. You can also segregate the scope of your web and mobile application using the same user pool.

In the next chapter, we will discuss the CI/CD approaches provided by AWS.

Points to remember

- Lambda authorizer is an API gateway feature to authorizer API using the Lambda function.

- AWS Cognito is a centralized, AWS-managed service for user management enabling the users to sign in through mobile and web.

- JWT is a modern approach to pass information for authorization as a JSON object.

- Cognito user pool is a user directory that will authenticate a user.

Multiple choice questions

1. **Which Cognito authentication flow is used for server-to-server communication?**
   a) ALLOW_ADMIN_USER_PASSWORD_AUTH
   b) ALLOW_CUSTOM_AUTH
   c) ALLOW_USER_PASSWORD_AUTH'

2. **Which Cognito authentication is used for client-side communication?**
   a) ALLOW_ADMIN_USER_PASSWORD_AUTH
   b) ALLOW_CUSTOM_AUTH
   c) ALLOW_USER_PASSWORD_AUTH

3. **Does Lambda authorizer pass ___ as a response in case of Success or Failure?**
   a) Token
   b) IAM policy
   c) None of these

Answer

1. a
2. c
3. b

CHAPTER 10

Continuous Integration and Deployment

You Build it, You Run it.

--- Werner Voegls – VP & CTO at Amazon.com

Introduction

Continuous Integration and Deployment (CI/CD) is the hottest topic in today's software industry. Every client wants a CI/CD pipeline for their project to be built upon so that they have full control over what and when the next releases will be deployed. This also gives power to developers who build the software and automate deployment using different CI/CD tools. Earlier, a separate team was assigned to big projects only for deployments and rollbacks in case of failure. Now, with the introduction and maturity of CI/CD tools, it is expected that every developer understands the process and is not dependent on any team. If the developers feel after proper regression testing that their software is good to be released, they only need to execute the pipeline. However, it is always a good practice to add lead or manager approval before deploying the release in production. CI/CD empowers the developers to decide on release without having to worry about rollback. If the current release fails, they can always quickly roll back to the previous version in no time. In this chapter, we will focus on how to create an AWS-provided CI/CD tool, that is, CodePipeline to deploy Lambda functions.

Structure

AWS CodePipeline

- Source
- Build
  - o Environment
  - o Buildspec
  - o Artifacts
  - o Configuring logs
- Deploy
- Execution
- PowerShell Script

Objective

After reading this chapter, you can create AWS CodePipeline, configure and deploy it. Use PowerShell scripts for quick deployment in the development environment.

In the end, you will be able to create your own AWS CodePipeline and work on it.

AWS CodePipeline

CodePipeline allows you to automate build, test, and deploy phases for your development environments. It helps you manage and release your software reliably and efficiently. CodePipeline uses stages to add AWS management tools, like **CodeCommit**, **CodeBuild**, and **CodeDeploy**. You can add a manual approval stage, in case someone needs to approve it before deploying, especially in a production environment. There are mainly three stages in the AWS CodePipeline – source, build and deploy. In this demo, we will use *GitHub* as a source.

The following diagram shows the different stages involved in AWS CodePipeline Lambda deployment:

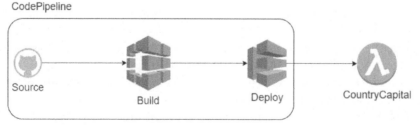

Figure 10.1: *AWS CodePipeline*

The following screenshot shows the creation of a new pipeline by going to AWS Console and then CodePipeline service. Specify pipeline name as countrycapital-pipeline and AWS will create a role name on your behalf:

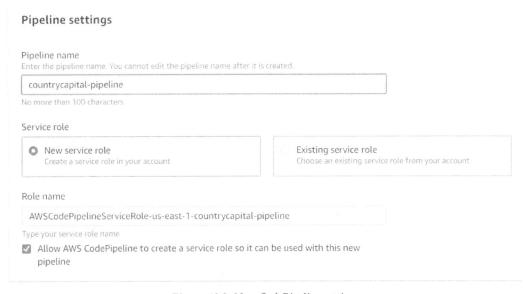

Figure 10.2: New CodePipeline settings

Source

AWS provides two options for source control: *AWS CodeCommit* and *GitHub*.

- AWS CodeCommit is one of the fully managed services provided by AWS to host and version control using Git. This will encrypt your code, both in transit as well as at rest. It will scale automatically as your source code grows and is highly available.

- *GitHub* is a subsidiary of *Microsoft* to host software and version control using *Git*.

In this demo, the *BPB GitHub* CountryCapital repository is used as a source and integrate with CodeBuild.

Follow these steps to integrate source with *GitHub*:

1. Under the Action Provider option, select **GitHub version 2**. If you are connecting a GitHub account for the first time, it will ask you to create a connection.

We have named the GitHub app connection **countrycapital-connection-string,** As shown in the following screenshot:

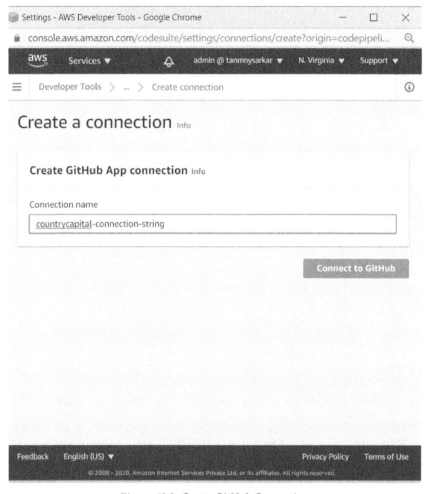

Figure 10.3: Create GitHub Connection

2. Next, click on **Connect to GitHub.** This will ask you to install a new app.

    We will click on the install app, As shown in the following screenshot:

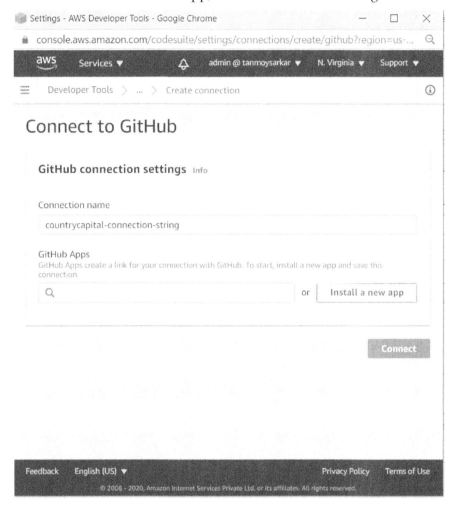

***Figure 10.4**: Install GitHub App*

3. As soon as you click on Install a new app, AWS will ask for permission.

    The following screenshot shows the option for authorization. Click on **Authorize AWS Connector for GitHub** option for AWS to create a connection on behalf of your application:

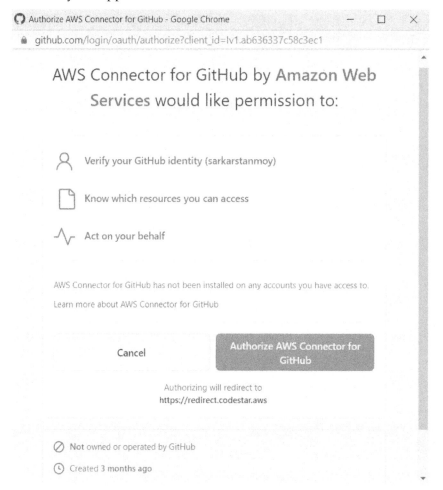

Figure 10.5: Authorize AWS Connector for GitHub

4. Once authorized, AWS will install the required connector.

The following screenshot shows the option where you can permit all the repositories or selected repository:

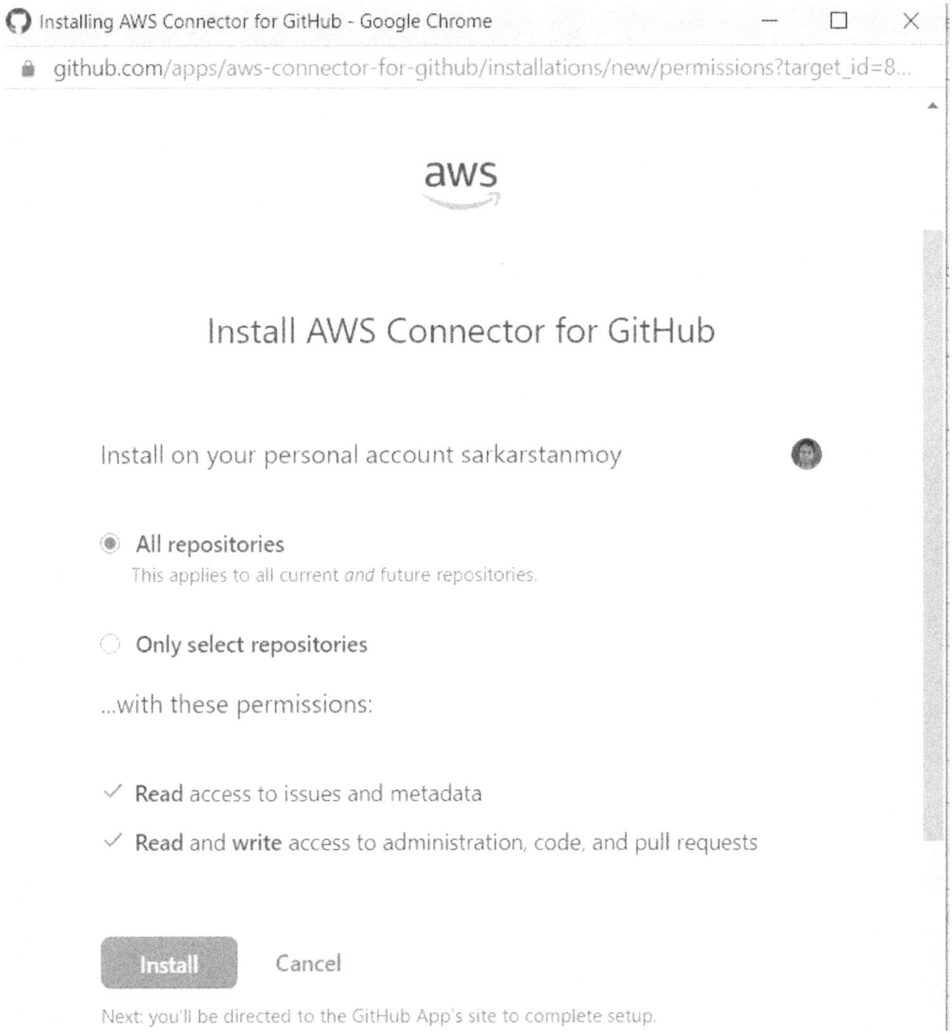

Figure 10.6: *Install AWS Connector for GitHub*

5. If everything is properly configured, your source will show Read to connect.

The following screenshot shows that the GitHub account has been successfully connected to the CodePipeline source stage:

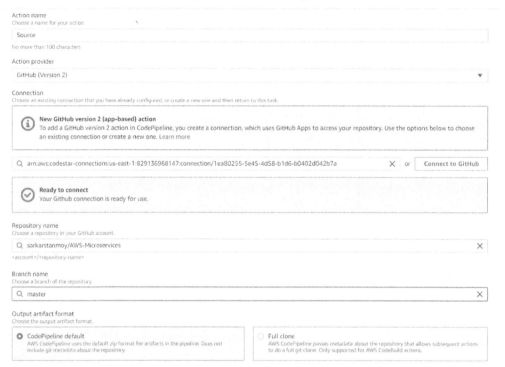

Figure 10.7: Source Configuration

Build

AWS CodeBuild is a fully managed build service that eliminates the need to manage and scale your build servers. CodeBuild can process multiple builds parallelly and charges by minute the compute resources are used.

To create a Build project, we will first start with creating a project by giving a valid name.

We have created a project named **countrycapital-build,** As shown in the following screenshot:

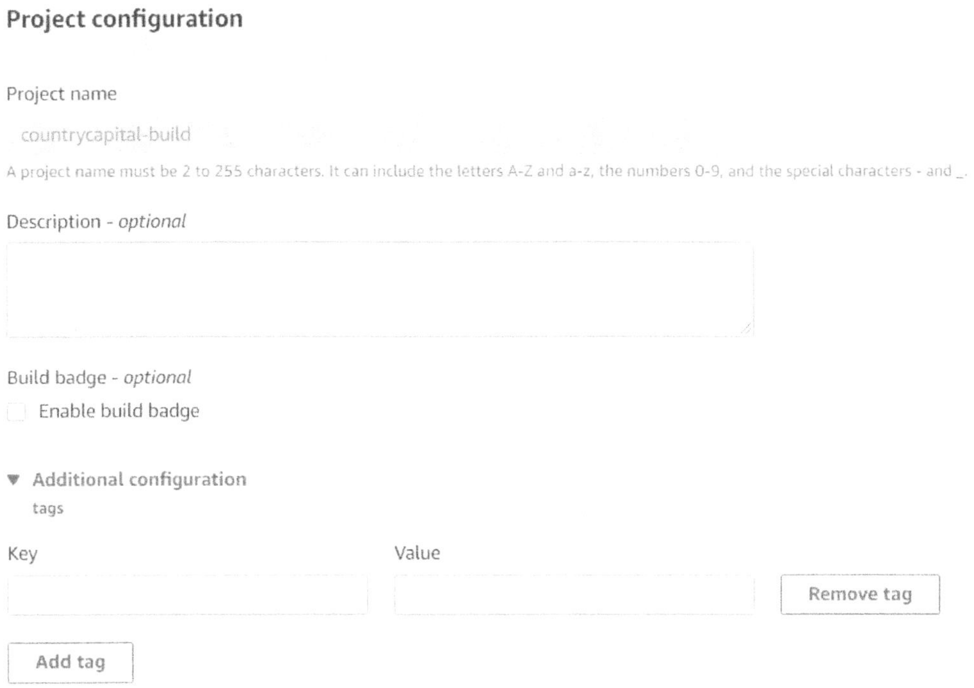

Project configuration

Project name

countrycapital-build

A project name must be 2 to 255 characters. It can include the letters A-Z and a-z, the numbers 0-9, and the special characters - and _.

Description - *optional*

Build badge - *optional*

☐ Enable build badge

▼ Additional configuration

tags

Key

Value

Remove tag

Add tag

Figure 10.8: *Build Project Configuration*

Environment

The environment settings are used to mention which environment your code will be built in.

I have used the Ubuntu Operating System (which is recommended) to build the code. AWS CodeBuild will provision a docker image with Ubuntu OS having programming runtime installed and build the code. You can also specify your custom IAM image in the case where you need additional software to build your application, as shown in the following screenshot:

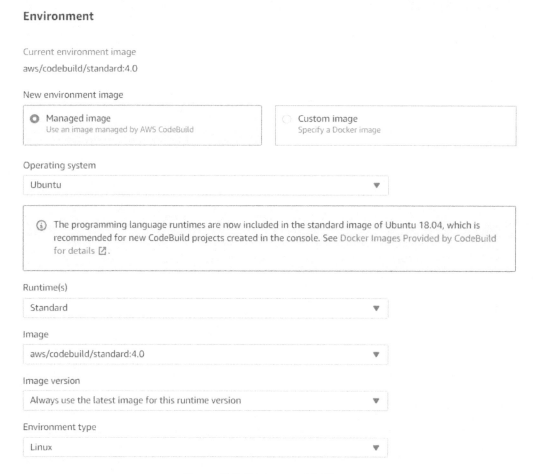

Figure 10.9: Environment Settings

Buildspec

Next, we must define the buildspec file which has commands to run while building your application.

Buildspec is a collection of build commands and settings in the YAML format used to build the project. Buildspec is also used to define parameter-store values and secret manager values to secure sensitive values. You can either use an inline *Buildspec* editor or create a **buildspec** file under the root of your application.

In the following code snippet, we have defined phases in the Buildspec file with a dedicated section for **pre_build, build,** and **post_build** commands. **Pre_build** is used to define commands before we start building our application as NuGet restore. Once **pre_build** completes, the actual build starts under the build phase. Finally, **post_build** is used to define the build packages and store them under the S3 buckets mentioned under artifacts. We need our artifacts to be zipped and then stored in S3. That's why the type of artifact is zip. Also, **outputtemplate.yaml** is under the files that we don't want to zip and move it as it is to S3. This is a SAM template and is used while deploying:

```
version: 0.2
phases:
  pre_build:
    commands:
      - echo Restore started on `date`
      - dotnet restore Chapter5/Microservices.CountryCapital/
Microservices.CountryCapital.API/Microservices.CountryCapital.API.csproj
  build:
    commands:
      - echo Build started on `date`
      - dotnet build Chapter5/Microservices.CountryCapital/
Microservices.CountryCapital.API/Microservices.CountryCapital.API.csproj
--configuration release
  post_build:
    commands:
      - echo 'Publish started'
      - dotnet publish -c Release -r win-x64 --self-contained false
Chapter5/Microservices.CountryCapital/Microservices.CountryCapital.API/
Microservices.CountryCapital.API.csproj
      - aws cloudformation package --template-file Chapter5/
Microservices.CountryCapital/Microservices.CountryCapital.API/bin/
Release/netcoreapp3.1/win-x64/publish/serverless.template --s3-bucket
countrycapital-cicd --output-template-file outputtemplate.yaml
artifacts:
  type: zip
  files:
    - outputtemplate.yaml
```

> **Note: Make sure to change the "Copy to Output Directory" property of the serverless.template to Always, if you notice the AWS cloud formation package command points to a serverless.template in the publish folder. The reason behind this is because the artifacts are zipped where serverless.template file is located and in this case, we need artifacts from the release folder.**

The following screenshot shows the insertion of the preceding **Buildspec** code in the AWS **CodePipeline** builds stage using the **Insert build** command option.

Another option is to use a **buildspec file**. To use this option, create a **buildpsec** (make sure to name the file **buildspec.yaml**) file in the YAML formatted file and place it in the root of the solution. AWS build will check for this file and if exists, it will execute it.

Figure 10.10: Buildspec commands

Artifacts

Create a new S3 bucket named **countrycapital-cicd** to store your build artifacts. For artifact packaging, you can either select none or zip. In the case of the zip option, your file will be compressed and stored as a ZIP file. Since we have already zipped our artifacts in buildspec we don't need to further zip it. Refer to the following screenshot:

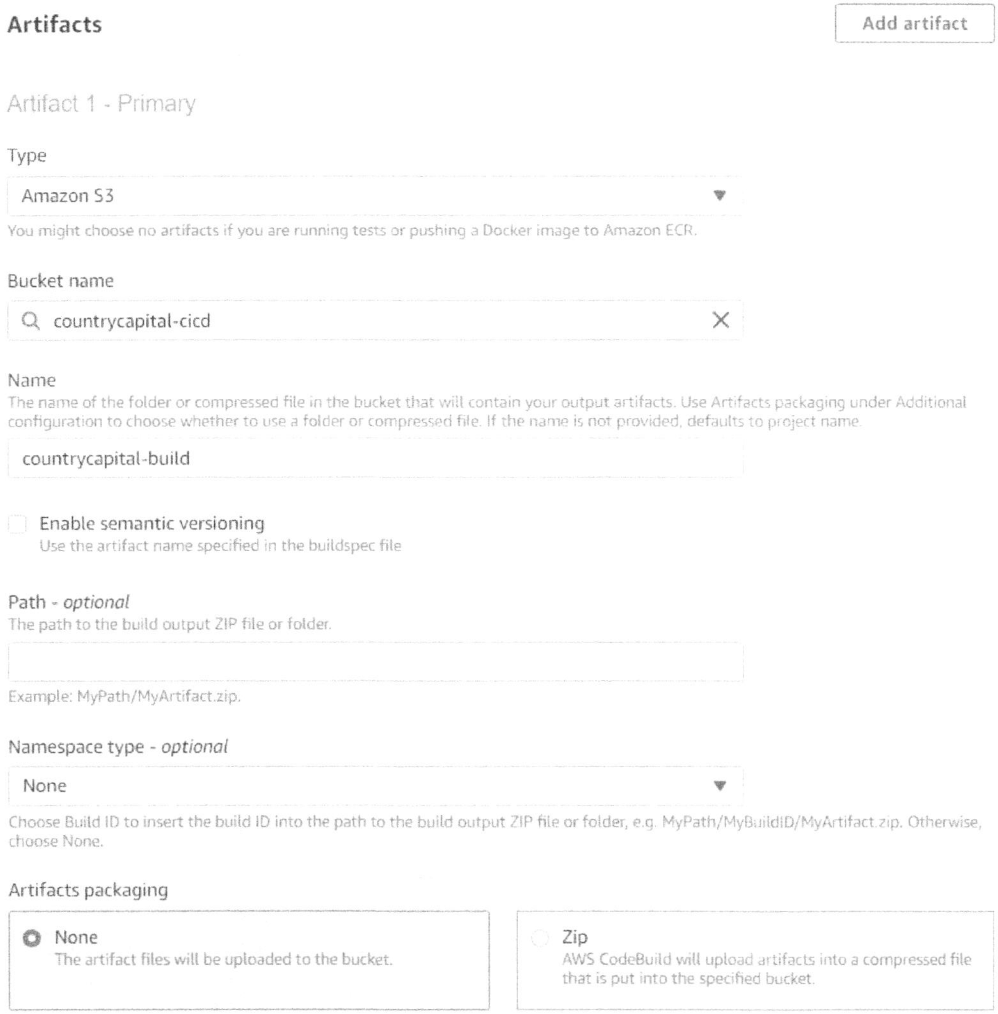

Artifacts

Add artifact

Artifact 1 - Primary

Type

Amazon S3	▼

You might choose no artifacts if you are running tests or pushing a Docker image to Amazon ECR.

Bucket name

Q countrycapital-cicd	✕

Name

The name of the folder or compressed file in the bucket that will contain your output artifacts. Use Artifacts packaging under Additional configuration to choose whether to use a folder or compressed file. If the name is not provided, defaults to project name.

countrycapital-build

☐ Enable semantic versioning
Use the artifact name specified in the buildspec file

Path - *optional*
The path to the build output ZIP file or folder.

Example: MyPath/MyArtifact.zip.

Namespace type - *optional*

None	▼

Choose Build ID to insert the build ID into the path to the build output ZIP file or folder, e.g. MyPath/MyBuildID/MyArtifact.zip. Otherwise, choose None.

Artifacts packaging

⦿ None	○ Zip
The artifact files will be uploaded to the bucket.	AWS CodeBuild will upload artifacts into a compressed file that is put into the specified bucket.

***Figure 10.11**: Configuring Build Artifacts*

Configuring logs

Finally, define logs that will store the logs of your build execution. This will help in identifying the issue in case the build fails. You can also persist your logs in S3 buckets. Refer to the following screenshot:

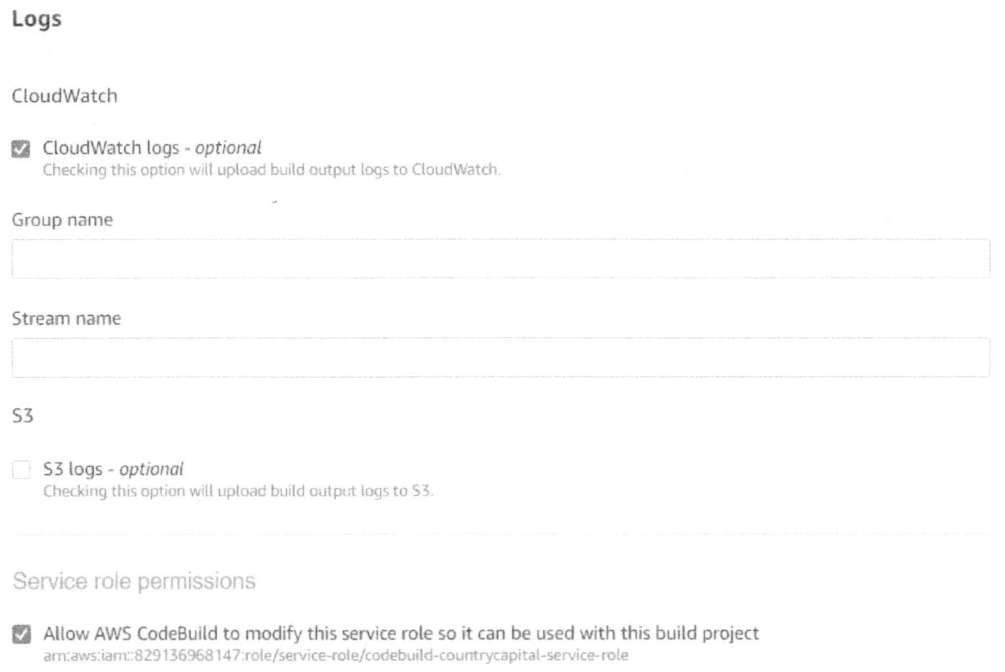

Logs

CloudWatch

☑ CloudWatch logs - *optional*
   Checking this option will upload build output logs to CloudWatch.

Group name

Stream name

S3

☐ S3 logs - *optional*
   Checking this option will upload build output logs to S3.

Service role permissions

☑ Allow AWS CodeBuild to modify this service role so it can be used with this build project
   arn:aws:iam::829136968147:role/service-role/codebuild-countrycapital-service-role

Figure 10.12: Configuring Build Logs

Deploy

The final stage of the pipeline is deployment. To deploy our Lambda functions, we will use AWS cloud formation as the deploy provider. Under BuildArtifcat, we will specify **outputtemplate.yaml** (SAM file in YAML format) file which we have generated at the build stage. The **outputtemplate.yaml** file contains the **CodeUri** property which will specify the location of the code to be deployed. Finally, select capabilities as **CAPABILITY_IAM** and **CAPABILITY_AUTO_EXPAND**. Capabilities allow cloud formation to create IAM resources on your behalf and provide proper permissions to create/update AWS resources. Refer to the following screenshot:

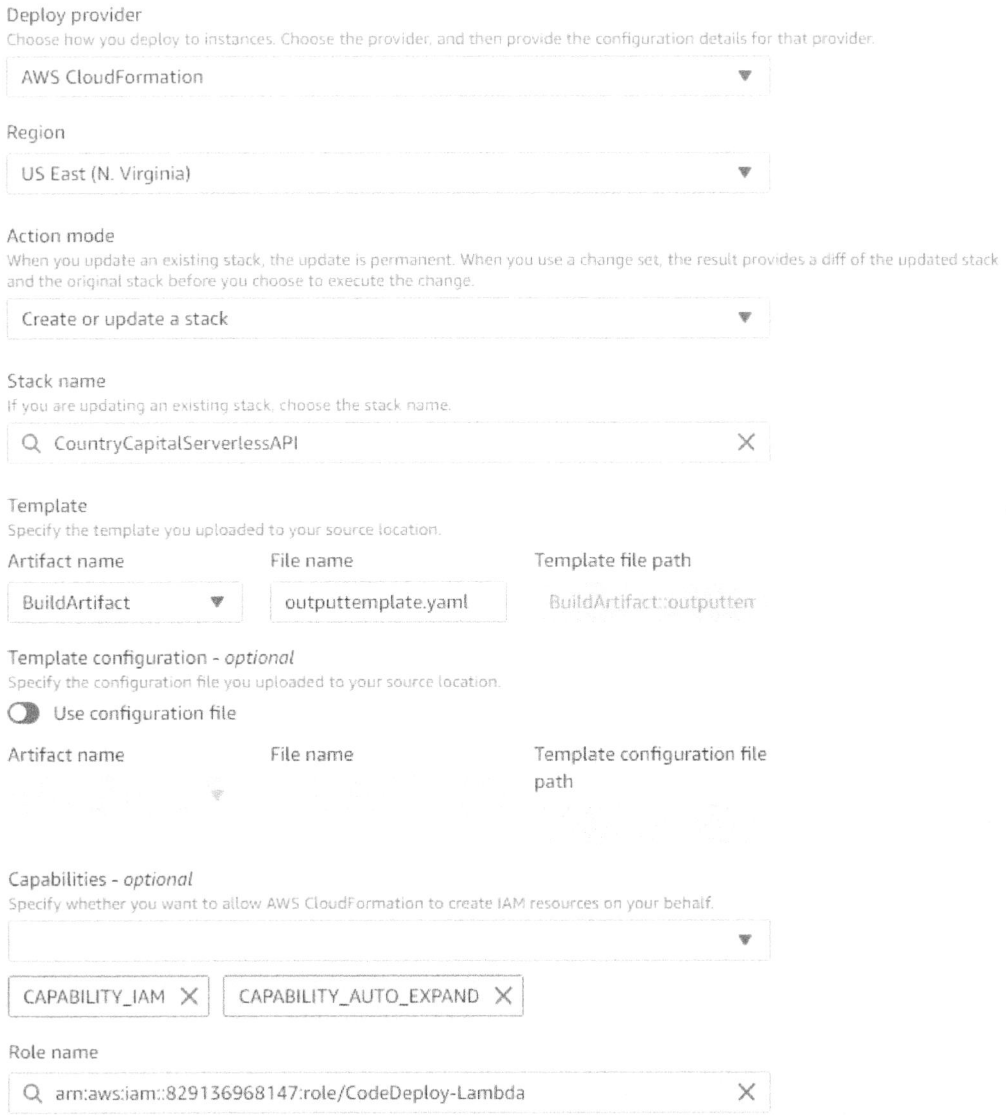

Deploy provider
Choose how you deploy to instances. Choose the provider, and then provide the configuration details for that provider.

AWS CloudFormation ▼

Region

US East (N. Virginia) ▼

Action mode
When you update an existing stack, the update is permanent. When you use a change set, the result provides a diff of the updated stack and the original stack before you choose to execute the change.

Create or update a stack ▼

Stack name
If you are updating an existing stack, choose the stack name.

Q CountryCapitalServerlessAPI ✕

Template
Specify the template you uploaded to your source location.

Artifact name	File name	Template file path
BuildArtifact ▼	outputtemplate.yaml	BuildArtifact::outputten

Template configuration - *optional*
Specify the configuration file you uploaded to your source location.

⬤ Use configuration file

Artifact name	File name	Template configuration file path

Capabilities - *optional*
Specify whether you want to allow AWS CloudFormation to create IAM resources on your behalf.

▼

CAPABILITY_IAM ✕   CAPABILITY_AUTO_EXPAND ✕

Role name

Q arn:aws:iam::829136968147:role/CodeDeploy-Lambda ✕

Figure 10.13: *Configuring Code Deploy*

Execution

If everything is configured properly, run your pipeline and it will show the success message at every stage. We have run the countrycapital pipeline and everything is green, as shown in the following screenshot:

Figure 10.14: Code Pipeline Execution

PowerShell script

Developing and testing Lambda functions on Windows PowerShell can be very handy for quick deployment and checking. Let me explain the following PowerShell command to deploy the **CountryCapital** Lambda function:

```
dotnet lambda deploy-serverless "CountryCapitalServerlessApi" -pl <<path
of serverless project>> --template serverless.template --region "us-
```

```
east-1" --profile <<AWS profile configured on your machine>> -c Release -f
netcoreapp3.1 -sb countrycapital-cicd
```

dotnet Lambda command is provided by AWS toolkit for Visual Studio to deploy .NET Core Lambda functions. The option **deploy-serverless** is used to specify that we are deploying AWS serverless applications by providing the name of the Lambda function. The command will create a new lambda function in case it is new or update if it already exists. Now, we must provide the path of the serverless project, template, the region to deploy your Lambda function, AWS profile which you have configured on your machine, define project configuration, framework, and finally, S3 bucket name (make sure the bucket exists where you will deploy your Lambda function).

The following screenshot shows the output of the PowerShell command:

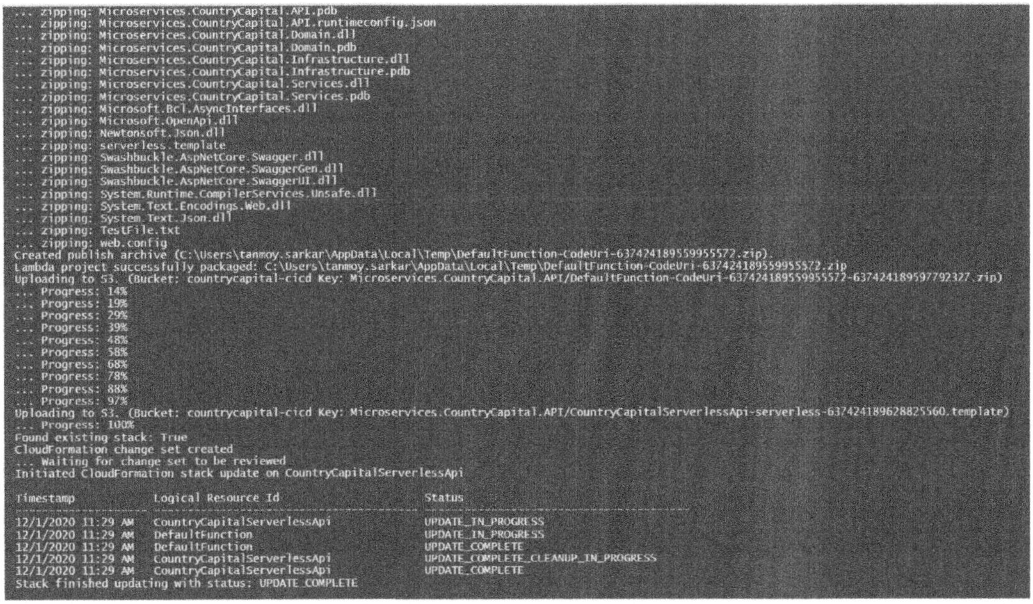

Figure 10.15: Lambda PowerShell command

Conclusion

Many organizations are adopting DevOps practices, which is a combination of practices and tools that increase the organization's ability to deploy services at a much higher rate. Serverless applications tied to DevOps allow the deployment of the code seamlessly without having to worry about other infrastructure changes whenever needed. With the introduction of AWS CodePipeline, it becomes much easier to configure, build, and deploy using the AWS ecosystem. In this chapter, we saw how to configure CodePipeline and use it for deployment.

In the next final chapter, we will discuss some of the best practices and tricks.

Points to remember

- CodePipeline allows you to automate build, test, and deploy phases.

- CodePipeline helps you manage and release your software reliably and efficiently.

- AWS CodeCommit is one of the fully managed services provided by AWS to host and version control using Git.

- GitHub is a subsidiary of Microsoft to host software and version control using Git.

- Buildspec is a collection of build commands and settings in the YAML format used to build the project.

- CodeUri property will specify the location of the code to be deployed.

- Windows PowerShell can be very handy for quick deployment and checking.

Multiple choice questions

1. What are the source controls currently supported by the AWS CodePipeline?
    a) GitHub
    b) SVN
    c) AWS CodeCommit

2. **Buildspec is a collection of build commands and settings in JSON format.**
    a) True
    b) False

3. **The minimum number of stages in the pipeline is 2 and the maximum is 10.**
    a) True
    b) False

Answer

1. a,c
2. b
3. a

CHAPTER 11

AWS Best Practices

> **Cloud is about how you do computing, not where you do computing.**
>
> *— Paul Maritz, CEO VMware*

Introduction

In the final chapter of this book, some best practices and tools are mentioned that will be used while working on provisioning microservices on Lambda. Without proper design and understanding, the limitations of AWS service can lead to unprecedented issues. You might become overwhelmed with the services provided by AWS and want to use them in your project. My suggestion is to always do some POC and find limitations before you incorporate these services in your design. Ask questions like do you really want this service without complicating the design. At the end of the day, if you make the design too complex, it will become difficult to maintain and error-prone to changes.

Structure

In this chapter, we will discuss the following topics:

Best practices

- Lambda payload limit

- Lambda cold-start

- Lambda layers

- API gateway response timeout

- Secret manager

- Create API versions

- Use step functions

- Use CI/CD pipeline

Objective

This chapter aims to provide some of the best practices of Lambda to use it in a project, some of the challenges you might encounter, and their resolutions. This chapter will also cover the services to consider when you architect microservices for AWS.

Best practices

Here are some of the best practices to keep in mind while you design microservices using Lambda. These practices will help you improve the performance, security, and easy deployment of your application.

Lambda payload limit

Lambda cannot handle the size of more than 6 MB of payload. Many developers, while they develop serverless API on AWS, don't come across this issue because initially, the request/response payload is low. But as the code becomes more mature and more data is squeezed in, the issues start to pop up, especially on response.

One of the solutions for this issue is data compression. In ASP.NET Core 3.1, the following steps help to incorporate changes required to implement compression:

- In Startup under **ConfigureServices,** add the following code. In the following code, we will use gzip compression to compress the response:

```
services.AddResponseCompression(options      =>{options.Providers.
Add<GzipCompressionProvider>();options.EnableForHttps = true;});
```

- Under the Configure method, we will inject the **UseResponseCompression** method in the ASP.NET Core middleware pipeline which will compress the response before sending it to the network:

```
app.UseResponseCompression();
```

- Now, in the Lambda function file under **Init** method, add **RegisterResponseContentEncodingForContentType** to register and initialize gzip encoding:

  ```
  RegisterResponseContentEncodingForContentType("application/
  json",ResponseContentEncoding.Base64);
  ```

- And finally, in the API gateway, select Lambda function and under settings, add Binary Media Types to "/" (make sure to add double quotes).

  If you call this API from any other Lambda function using HTTP client, make sure to add gzip network handler to HTTP client handler:

  ```
  HttpClientHandler handler = new HttpClientHandler()

  {

  AutomaticDecompression=DecompressionMethods.GZip|
  DecompressionMethods.Deflate

  };
  using (var client = new HttpClient(handler)) {

  var response = await client.SendAsync(requestMessage);

  }
  ```

Lambda cold-start

Lambda cold-start is typically the overhead while we execute Lambda functions. It consists of two parts, the setup execution environment and the code initialization duration. This can significantly affect the performance of your API hosted in a serverless application. Since the setup execution environment is fully managed by AWS, we can only control the code initialization duration.

One solution to keep Lambda warm all the time is to create a health endpoint and create a CloudWatch event that will trigger the health interval on a scheduled time interval.

Another option that can be used is to use Lambda provisioned concurrency. In the provisioned concurrency, you can define the number of Lambda function instances you want to keep running to avoid a cold-start delay for the client.

Lambda layers

While you deploy Lambda functions, the code will be zipped and stored in S3. Every time a new instance of Lambda function runs, it will start a new execution environment and copy the code from the S3 bucket. If the size of the code is very big, it will take time to copy and provision it into the execution environment.

In order to reduce the size of the code and increase the performance, we can use Lambda layers. However, you can use up to 5 layers at a time in your serverless application.

API gateway response timeout

The API gateway has a response limit of 30 seconds. If your API doesn't reply in 30 seconds, then it might return 500 errors, based on the configuration. Multiple factors might increase the response time.

Since most of the heavy lifting is taken care of by the API gateway, when we host our API using it, it is recommended to follow some best practices mentioned here concerning Lambda to reduce the provision and execution time.

Lambda hosting strategies

As we already discussed, private subnets are the subnets that don't have access to the internet. Private subnets have a NAT gateway attached to them so that communication can be initiated within the subnet but not from the internet. Host your Lambda inside VPC if you want your Lambda to access private resources. When the Lambda function is not configured to connect to your VPC, it can access any public resources, like endpoints outside AWS services.

HTTP2 protocol

HTTP2 is a major revision of HTTP 1.0 and is used to improve the performance, speed, and efficiency of the web. Some of the improvements are as follows:

- A single connection is used to load the website and that connection will be active if the website is open. This reduces the overhead of multiple TCP connections.

- Header compression reduces the size of the overall payload in bytes during the communication. Also, it needs to be sent only once during the entire connection which significantly improves the performance of the application

- A binary protocol reduces the webpage overhead by encoding data into binary.

- The server push will push additional cacheable information to the client for future requests.

Secret manager

In one of my projects, we used parameter stores to store our sensitive data, like database usernames and passwords. However, at that time, the parameter store had a limitation of 40 keys/sec and when the load increased, our API began to fail because of this.

A secret manager is one of the options to store sensitive data and reference it under a Lambda environment. Using the secret manager, you can securely store, manage, and audit secrets used to access AWS resources.

Create API versions

Change is constant in microservice, and CI/CD helps the development team to quickly deploy the changes seamlessly. However, while we change the existing API contracts, we should be careful not to break the existing system using the API.

API versioning comes to the rescue when you change the contract of the existing API but doesn't want to break the applications using the old API contracts.

Use step functions

In the application, there are situations when we want to update different domain data for a request. Suppose a user completed the payment for an order. Once the payment is completed, the order API should be called to change the status of the order. Here, logistics API is called to start processing the order. To achieve these transactions, we can call the endpoint of different domains synchronously, which might lead to an issue, in case any one of the systems is slow.

It is always a good approach to orchestrate these transactions using step functions and manage them efficiently.

Use CI/CD pipeline

It is a good practice to create a CI/CD pipeline for your projects. In this book, we have discussed the AWS CodePipeline which should use while deploying the code in Lambda rather than doing the manual deployment. It will automate your deployment, run test cases, and standardize the process.

Open data protocol

Open Data Protocol (OData) is an application-level protocol for interacting with the data via the REST interface. Using OData, you can expose the database via REST endpoint to the client and the client can query the data using the custom OData query options. The advantage of this approach is that it reduces the number of endpoints by using the OData query options. However, it incurs extra responsibility to write an efficient query to avoid unnecessary data which can eventually lead to a heavy payload. So, it is always recommended to add projection to your OData query. Projection means the client should specify the fields which are needed from the OData endpoint for processing.

Stored procedures

As per microservices design, shared database is considered an anti-pattern. Most of the time, in the case of brownfield application and sometimes in the greenfield application, shared database comes to the rescue. Initially, when we don't have enough business knowledge to segregate the data, it is wise to use a shared database. However, design your application in a way such that in the future, when you segregate the database, it will have minimum side effects. In some scenarios, the client wants the aggregated data from the endpoint, which may take more time than expected, trying to process in-memory using the ORM. So, creating store procedures is an efficient solution to aggregate the data and send it back to the client.

CloudWatch log messages

CloudWatch is the centralized logging platform for AWS where the AWS services log their information. When designing microservice, make sure to log information in a proper format to leverage cloud formation search queries. In most applications, we usually store information in JSON format to search for information.

Rate limit

ASP.NET Core allows you to put a rate limit to your endpoint to reduce unnecessary traffic. You can apply rules like the request from an IP cannot be more than 5 requests/sec. In this way, it will restrict the malicious clients to overload your backend with unnecessary requests.

Conclusion

Issues like Lambda cold-start, API gateway response timeout limit, etc. can significantly affect the overall performance of your application. It is always wise to address these issues from the beginning of the project and create a guideline. In this chapter, we discussed some of the important practices to follow in order to improve the overall performance and security of your application.

With this chapter, I am concluding this book. In this book, we went through the implementation of microservices using Lambda and found that serverless applications cannot only be used to respond to events but can also be used to host complex backend processing. The best part is that you don't have to manage it. It's cost-effective and can focus solely on your code.

Thanks for bearing with me throughout this journey. I hope you have gathered enough knowledge to start with provisioning microservice on Lambda.

Points to remember

- Lambda cannot handle the size of more than 6 MB of payload.

- Lambda cold-start is typically overhead while we execute the Lambda functions. It consists of two parts, the setup execution environment and the code initialization duration.

- To reduce the size of the code and increase the performance, we can use Lambda layers.

- API gateway has a response limit of 30 seconds.

- Using the secret manager, you can securely store, manage, and audit secrets used to access AWS resources.

- Use API cersioning when you want to change the contract of the existing API but don't want to break the applications using the old API contracts.

Multiple choice questions

1. **Lambda payload size limit is ___?**
   a) 8MB
   b) 6 MB
   c) 1 GB

2. **To reduce Lambda cold-start, use:**
   a) Lambda layers
   b) CloudWatch events
   c) All the above

3. **API gateway has a response limit of ___:**
   a) 10 sec
   b) 30 sec
   c) 1 min

Answer

1. b
2. c
3. b

Index

Made in the USA
Las Vegas, NV
24 October 2021

33020095R00116